"The thing about the psalms is this: they are so human and they meet us where we're at while also grabbing our eyes and putting them on heaven. This book by Laura L. Smith *will* restore your soul, because it's God's promises meeting human emotions. You can be exactly where you're at and get all of God—this is the good news for women like us."

Jess Connolly, church leader, author of 9 books including *You Are the Girl for the Job*, and founder and CEO of Go & Tell Gals

"In addition to shaping, supporting, and providing wings for our faith, the Psalms help us align our thinking and emotions to the mind and heart of God. In these 150 Spirit-inspired prayers, we have been given a treasure chest of what it looks like not only to love God with our minds (sound theology) but also to love Him with heart, soul, and strength (robust and awakened living). Using thirty of the Psalms' 'greatest hits' as her guide, Laura helps us use Psalms as our top-shelf resource for loving God and becoming more fully human. I highly recommend this work to you."

Scott Sauls, senior pastor of Christ Presbyterian Church and author of several books including *Jesus Outside the Lines* and *Beautiful People Don't Just Happen*

"In *Restore My Soul*, Laura L. Smith lays out the most beautiful of invitations. As she shares her own stories of learning to weave the Psalms into her own prayer life, we too are welcomed to bring our confused, weary, hurting selves to God. Whether you're taking your very first steps in exploring life with God or have walked with Him for years, you will find day-by-day direction and encouragement with Laura as your friendly and gentle guide through some of the Bible's most beloved psalms."

Bronwyn Lea, author of *Beyond Awkward Side Hugs*; editorial curator at Propel Women

"Laura L. Smith dives into the richness of Psalms in a fresh way by sharing honest stories, joys, and struggles, as if you were chatting over a cup of coffee, all the while leading you closer to the love and grace God has waiting for you."

Elisa Morgan, speaker; author of
When We Pray Like Jesus; cohost of *Discover the Word*
and *God Hears Her*; president emerita of MOPS International

CONTENTS

RESTORE my SOUL

The Power *and* Promise *of* 30 Psalms

LAURA L. SMITH

Our Daily Bread
Publishing™

Restore My Soul: The Power and Promise of 30 Psalms

© 2022 by Laura L. Smith

Requests for permission to quote from this book should be directed to: Permissions Department, Our Daily Bread Publishing, PO Box 3566, Grand Rapids, MI 49501, or contact us by email at permissionsdept@odb.org.

Interior design by Michael J. Williams

Library of Congress Cataloging-in-Publication Data

Names: Smith, Laura L., 1969- author.

Title: Restore my soul : the power and promise of 30 Psalms / Laura L. Smith.

Description: Grand Rapids, MI : Our Daily Bread Publishing, [2022] | Includes bibliographical references. | Summary: "Dive into the power of the Psalms and be inspired to praise God as you read Restore My Soul: The Power and Promise of 30 Psalms"-- Provided by publisher.

Identifiers: LCCN 2021060629 | ISBN 9781640701625

Subjects: LCSH: Bible. Psalms--Criticism, interpretation, etc. | BISAC: RELIGION / Christian Living / Devotional | RELIGION / Biblical Meditations / Old Testament

Classification: LCC BS1430.52 .S644 2022 | DDC 223/.206--dc23/eng/20220506

LC record available at https://lccn.loc.gov/2021060629

Printed in the United States of America

23 24 25 26 27 28 29 30 / 9 8 7 6 5 4 3 2

For my mom. Thank you for teaching me
how to laugh and cry. For showing me
it's okay to feel joy and pain. And mostly
for shining the light of Jesus everywhere you go.

INTRODUCTION

Songs? Poems? Curses? Prayers? Laments? Tear-filled pleadings? Rejoicings? The Psalms are all these things. Just like the music played on the radio today is a mishmash of songs written with the purpose of getting you to dance or weep or contemplate, the music of the Bible, much of which has been organized into the book of Psalms, is the cry of people's hearts—at our best and at our worst. And because humankind has always celebrated and mourned, loved and hated, danced and begged in desperation, the Psalms still ring true today, touching the gamut of human emotions and experiences.

Join me in these pages as we explore how these songs written thousands of years ago can still help us no matter what we're going through, because they point us back to our good, faithful, powerful, and loving God.

1

BETTER THAN SELF-HELP

Psalm 1

Blessed is the one
  who does not walk in step with the wicked
or stand in the way that sinners take
  or sit in the company of mockers,
but whose delight is in the law of the L<small>ORD</small>,
  and who meditates on his law day and
      night.
That person is like a tree planted by streams
      of water,
  which yields its fruit in season
and whose leaf does not wither—
  whatever they do prospers.

Not so the wicked!
  They are like chaff
  that the wind blows away.
Therefore the wicked will not stand in the
      judgment,
  nor sinners in the assembly of the righteous.

For the L<small>ORD</small> *watches over the way of the*
      righteous,
  but the way of the wicked leads to
      destruction.

Live your best life! Break free! Reduce stress! Upgrade your brain! Defy the odds! Embrace who you are!

The top-selling self-help books promise you all this and more. Which sounds amazing. So amazing that approximately 18.6 million self-help books are sold each year,[1] and this number is growing, increasing 63 percent in January 2021 over January 2020![2]

Life is complicated and busy and uncertain. We want happiness. And we will try almost any secret sauce to get it. A gluten-free (or low-carb or higher-protein) diet, a new exercise program, essential oils. If they'll help us sleep better, get ahead, have healthier relationships, and feel more balanced? Sign us up. We keep trying new and better and harder, but some days we can't help but feel like something is missing.

Long before self-help books dominated Amazon, God offered to help us live our best lives. He still does. One where we can overcome obstacles, find peace in the midst of chaos, experience joy, understand what it feels like to be truly loved, and do amazing things He's already equipped us to do. It's way better than self-help could ever be. God's offer can restore our souls.

So what's the secret? How do we sign up?

In the very first psalm, God gives us the answer.

Psalm 1 was intentionally placed at the front of the book of Psalms, not because it was written first but to show us why we should read, sing, and meditate on the Psalms. Why do they matter? What is their purpose? How will they benefit us?

Ready?

> Blessed is the one . . .
>   who meditates on [God's] law day and
>   night.
> That person is like a tree planted by streams
>   of water,

which yields its fruit in season
and whose leaf does not wither. (Psalm
1:1–3)

I love *The Message* paraphrase of this passage:

You thrill to GOD's Word,
    you chew on Scripture day and night.
You're a tree replanted in Eden,
    bearing fresh fruit every month,
Never dropping a leaf,
    always in blossom. (vv. 2–3)

There it is. All in two verses. The secret to living an extraordinary life? Meditating on and thrilling in God's words.

So let's talk about God's Word, so we can thrill on it.

1. God's words are the Scriptures. At the time the psalmist wrote Psalm 1, Scripture consisted of the first five books of what we now call the Bible, written by Moses. We have the gift of the Bible in its entirety—yes, the original books of Moses the psalmist knew but also the words God spoke to His people through the prophets, the recordings of Jesus's life, and the letters to the early church. As 2 Timothy 3:16 tells us, "All Scripture is God-breathed." It shows us who God is, how He relates to His people, and how He longs to redeem us.

2. God's Word is also Jesus himself. The apostle John explains it like this:

In the beginning was the Word, and the Word was with God, and the Word was God. He was with God in the beginning. Through him all things were made; without him nothing was made that has been made. In him was life, and that life was the light of all mankind. . . .

The Word became flesh and made his dwelling among us. We have seen his glory, the glory of the one and only Son, who came from the Father, full of grace and truth. (John 1:1–4, 14)

God's *words* are in the Bible and Jesus is *the Word*. Basically, reading about Jesus in the Bible helps us understand Him, which helps us thrill in Him. When we truly make this our focus, we will bear fresh fruit. Which isn't language we typically use today, but it's basically what all those self-help books are promising, only better—fruitful lives. If we were an apple tree, this would be our main goal. We'd want to be blossoming and producing fruit. All. Of. The. Time. And not just any fruit. Sweet, juicy, delicious fruit. The apples that are crisp on the very first bite and that you want to crunch all the way down to the core.

So what does being fruitful mean for you and me?

People who focus on God's words say things that matter, take time for others, speak life and light into dark situations, and stand up for people who can't stand up for themselves. They bear fruit. Husbands and wives who focus on Jesus try their best to love one another selflessly, as Jesus loved them. Their marriages are fruitful. Artists and entrepreneurs who tap into the Creator's creativity paint beautiful murals, write songs that touch hearts, brew frothy cappuccinos, and design the parts that make up the cars, coffee makers, and containers we rely on. They produce beautiful and functional fruit for all of us to benefit from. People who do the work God has called them to do are fair to their employees and customers and coworkers. They're respectful to their bosses, use their time well, have meaningful friendships, and make a difference in the spaces they inhabit. They're fruitful.

Bearing fruit might not be the first way we'd describe an exuberant life. But it's how Jesus described it: "I am the vine; you are the branches. If you remain in me and I in you, you will *bear much fruit*; apart from me you can do nothing. . . . This is to my Father's glory, that *you bear much fruit*, showing yourselves to be my disciples. As the Father has loved me, so have I loved you. Now remain in my love" (John 15:5, 8–9, emphasis added).

If you remain in me and I in you, you will bear much fruit.

If we stay with Jesus, in the love and grace He offers, making Him our home, then we can bear not just some fruit—but much fruit. We can lead, be brave, stop worrying, think big, move forward, love, find peace, be disciplined and positive, make things happen, be whole again—basically the things those self-help books promise but don't always deliver.

Staying with Jesus? Simple, right?

Easy? Not necessarily.

Are we willing to incorporate consistently reading the Bible and praying (the two ways to meditate on the Word) into our busy, demanding lives? To take the steps and time that are required? I promise the fruit will be worth the fertilizing and weeding. But more importantly than anything I have to say is that Jesus promises it will be worth it.

And let's be honest, those self-help books require us to do things that take time and commitment. They might suggest we wake up earlier, switch to a vegan diet, or do sit-ups and make our beds every morning, and we're willing to try those things in order to reap the rewards. But their promises, although often good and helpful, feel shallow compared to the deep, rich life Jesus promises. If we're willing to try things for a self-help strategy, shouldn't we be willing to try things to experience this abundant, fruit-filled life Jesus offers?

The author of Psalm 1 gives us a gorgeous word picture of what it looks like to remain in God's words, to let the truth of Scripture sink into our hearts.

> That person is like a tree planted by streams
> of water,
> which yields its fruit in season
> and whose leaf does not wither—
> whatever they do prospers. (v. 3)

If we're seeking Jesus, reading the Bible on a regular basis to learn more about Him, and talking to Jesus (that's what prayer is), we're like trees planted by streams of water. We have a constant source of nutrition and hydration. Even during a dry spell, our roots can stretch out to that stream and draw enough life-giving love that we can continue. It's the fact that the tree is planted by streams of water that gives it life. Not that the tree has the biggest watering can, longest hose, or snazziest sprinkler system. That tree could be tall or short, have a thin or thick trunk, be good for climbing or shade or for birds to make their nests in or for producing maple syrup. None of those things make it blessed or not blessed. What makes that tree healthy and able to stand up to whatever storm or drought comes its way and capable of producing fruit is that it lives by the stream where water constantly flows.

Jesus said, "Let anyone who is thirsty come to me and drink. Whoever believes in me, as Scripture has said, rivers of living water will flow from within them" (John 7:37–38).

This stream we're supposed to park ourselves next to? It's Jesus! And our roots can sip His sweet water all day long. He never runs dry. We'll never thirst. We can obtain this amazing, fruitful life just by staying with Jesus and tapping into the nourishment He offers. This takes some intentionality, but it's so worth it.

Are we living by Jesus, hydrating ourselves with His living water?

The more we chew on God's words as Psalm 1 instructs, the more we'll discover how the words within the Bible's pages work together to tell one incredible story—one of a God who loves His people and wants to rescue and restore them. The psalmist says we'll be fruitful if we meditate on God's words. Jesus says we'll be fruitful if we remain in Him. This sounds exactly like the stream I want to be planted near.

We can start right now—drinking from the stream that is Jesus, the living water.

So grab your favorite water bottle or cutest mug. Fill it up. Get ready to drink in truth and love and grace that will not just sustain you but allow you to bear much fruit, to live your very best life.

--- RESTORE ---

Let's start this book with a look at our faith lives. This is for you, so be honest with yourself. How often do you read the Bible?

How often do you pray?

If you'd like to increase the amount of time or frequency you read the Bible or pray, set a measurable, attainable goal for yourself right now by writing it down here.

I find the more time I spend with Jesus, the more time I want to spend with Him. Because when I hang out with the Lord, I am more at peace. I find more joy. I have more courage. And those things feel so good. I'm praying for you on this journey through the Psalms—praying that you'll discover the love and grace Jesus so abundantly offers and that you will cease being thirsty and begin bearing much fruit.

2

YOU HAVE AUTHORITY

Psalm 8

LORD, our Lord,
how majestic is your name in all the earth!

You have set your glory
in the heavens.
Through the praise of children and infants
you have established a stronghold against
your enemies,
to silence the foe and the avenger.
When I consider your heavens,
the work of your fingers,
the moon and the stars,
which you have set in place,
what is mankind that you are mindful of
them,
human beings that you care for them?

You have made them a little lower than the
angels
and crowned them with glory and honor.
You made them rulers over the works of your
hands;
you put everything under their feet:
all flocks and herds,
and the animals of the wild,
the birds in the sky,

and the fish in the sea,
all that swim the paths of the seas.

LORD, *our Lord,*
how majestic is your name in all the earth!

W*ho would want to hear what you have to say about that?*
This is the lie in my head I often hear when I'm about to write a chapter, blog, or article. I hear it as I slide on my headset and test my microphone to begin a podcast interview or speak on a stage. Some days it makes me hesitate. It's a wrestling match with the repeated lie Satan whispers to me—"You're not good enough"—and the truth that Christ says, "You are enough." Scripture tells us God's people are His prized possessions, His master-pieces, His beloved, His royal priesthood (1 Peter 2:9). I know this; I believe this. And yet that sneaky snake slithers around my ankles and tries to tell me otherwise.

What has God commissioned *you* to do?

Teach a class? Take a class? Write a song? Perform a song? Stand up for the person no one else sees, or the one everyone not only sees but picks on? Join a committee to make a change in a broken system? Start a running club, book club, meal-delivery program, babysitting service, or ministry in your community? And the next question: What's stopping you?

Who would listen to what you have to say?
Who would want to hear it?
What if they don't like it?
Have you heard similar lies?

When I hear these untruths, it makes me pause and wonder and check my email and my likes on social media, trying to justify that maybe someone likes me and my words, that maybe, hopefully, my words are making a difference. As if the internet could measure how well we're doing what God created you or me to do.

It can't.

God is the only one who can. And when we follow His instructions, He's always pleased.

These doubts of our abilities or credibility don't affect just me and the rest of us "regular folks." Or people in our day and age. Even the famous Queen Esther, who has an entire book of the Bible devoted to her story, doubted if she should speak up, if her voice mattered.

Esther was an orphaned Jewish girl chosen out of all the young women in the 127 provinces of the Persian Empire to be the new bride for King Xerxes (Esther 2:3). When Xerxes's advisor Haman suggested the king murder everyone under his rule who was Jewish (3:9), Esther's cousin Mordecai tried to convince her that she, as queen, was in a position to stand up for their people (4:8).

But Esther was terrified to speak. And rightly so. Anyone who approached the king without being summoned would be sentenced to death (v. 11). Yeah, this even applied to the queen.

Sure, Queen Esther was Xerxes's favorite of all his wives and concubines, but he had so many. And the king hadn't even talked to Esther in over a month. Esther tried to explain all this to Mordecai. She worried that even if by some crazy circumstance the king granted her permission to speak, he would never listen to her about his political and military decisions. She wasn't qualified in any way. Her job was to please the king, not advise him.

And so the voices in our heads speak.

This is where Mordecai pushed back on Esther's insecurities and dropped his famous line on her, "Who knows if perhaps you were made queen for just such a time as this?" (v. 14 NLT).

Perhaps you too were put exactly where you are today, given the skill set you have, been introduced to the people you know, or placed in your apartment building or office or school by the God of the universe for such a time as this!

After fasting for three days, Esther got the courage to enter the king's court and speak. But in the moment when Xerxes asked, "What would you like?" the doubts flooded Esther again. Can you relate? Instead of making her request, Esther invited the king to dinner. At dinner Esther chickened out again. Instead of saying what she needed to say, Esther invited Xerxes to dinner a second time. What was the voice inside telling Esther? What made her stop short three times of saying what she felt passionate about even when Xerxes was listening?

What's stopping you?

On the second dinner date Esther finally got up the nerve to use her voice: "Then Queen Esther answered, 'If I have found favor with you, Your Majesty, and if it pleases you, grant me my life—this is my petition. And spare my people—this is my request. For I and my people have been sold to be destroyed, killed and annihilated'" (7:3–4).

And . . . the king sent out a new edict which protected the Jews. Esther's words were the catalyst that saved all the Jewish people in Persia from being massacred. And to think, she was this close to not going through with it. But as Psalm 8 reminds us, God is mindful of His people; He cares for them (v. 4). And He'll call you to do things to join in His marvelous, caring work.

All of us will doubt. Because of our position in life. Because of past experiences. Because of what we think it takes to say or do the thing. Because of what they told us.

The enemy knows this and whispers—"Why you? Why do you think you could do this? There are risks involved, you know. Why would they listen? Won't you be embarrassed? What if it doesn't work?"

Because Esther overcame her doubts and spoke up, the Jewish nation was saved. Her voice really did matter.

And so does yours! The world needs to hear, be with, and learn from you too. Psalm 8 says God created you, crowned you, and made you a ruler. C'mon now!

> What is mankind that you [God] are mindful
>   of them,
>   human beings that you care for them?
>
> You have made them a little lower than the
>   angels
>   and crowned them with glory and honor.
> You made them rulers over the works of your
>   hands;
>   you put everything under their feet.
>   (vv. 4–6)

John, who calls himself "the disciple Jesus loved," tells us, "The Spirit who lives in you is greater than the spirit who lives in the world" (1 John 4:4 NLT). God put the Holy Spirit, who is greater than anything going on in this world, within us. God crowned us with glory and honor and made us rulers of His creation, and we're hesitant to try out, apply, step up, write it down, or send that email?

Yeah.

Me too sometimes.

But then I remember that Jesus has shared His authority with me to do the things He asks me to do! He's done the same for you. It's not all up to us. All Esther had to do was approach the king and ask. If God asks me to write or speak about Him, I'm supposed to do exactly that. Even if I'm having the worst hair day. Even if I'm nervous. Even if I'm not fluent in New Testament Greek. I'm supposed to share a biblical truth, and God will make sure the people He wants to hear it will hear it.

It's simpler than we make it. We put pressure on ourselves for all the outcomes when that's God's job. He's more than capable of handling the results.

How might God be calling you to use the authority He's given you? To focus on input, on what you can do? This could be done a billion different ways. It could mean pursuing your dream of becoming an actor and one day sharing your faith during an interview with Jimmy Fallon. It could mean taking brownies to your neighbor who had surgery and taping a note that says "I'm praying for you" to the plastic wrap protecting the fudgy goodness. Or coaching a softball team using Christian principles, letting those young athletes know why you think it's important to love one another on and off the field.

It does *not* mean allowing the voice in your head to talk you out of chasing your acting dream if you feel God has given you this passion, or shaming your athletes, or not writing that note because you're worried about what other people will think.

Jesus doesn't promise that everyone will like it when we do what He's called us to do. But that was never the point. As Paul tells the church in Thessalonica: "We speak as those approved by God to be entrusted with the gospel. We are not trying to please people but God, who tests our hearts" (1 Thessalonians 2:4).

The point is that when we do the things Jesus calls us to do, He's our audience, our committee, our customer— not the world. Jesus jumps up and down and cheers when we act on the things He puts in our hearts. He throws His head back and laughs with glee. Jesus pumps His fist and says, "Way to go!" Jesus isn't disappointed or embarrassed but delighted. If anything, He asks, "What took you so long?"

Who would listen?

Who would want it?

What if they don't like it?

The questions the world, the enemy, and even our own brains ask are decoys from what truly matters.

What if we replied, "Who cares?" And then recited the truths of Psalm 8 as a reminder, "I'm crowned with glory and honor. I'm a ruler over God's creation. God put everything under my feet!"

God asked a man named Joshua to knock down a city wall by marching around it for seven days. Actually two walls. The outer wall of Jericho was thirty feet high and six feet thick. The inner wall was also thirty feet high and twelve feet thick! I'm guessing some of Joshua's army, and perhaps a couple of the priests he asked to march with him, questioned this strategy. They might have said, "Why, again, do you think walking in circles around a city will take down those mighty walls?"

Joshua didn't have a bulldozer or a wrecking ball, but Joshua had God's authority to make those walls come tumbling down (Joshua 6). He acted on it, and they fell.

God gave an unwed teenage girl named Mary the power and authority to have a baby who would become our Savior, Jesus Christ (Matthew 1; Luke 1). Keep in mind that Mary hadn't had intercourse or in vitro, she wasn't a priest or a rabbi, but God gave her the authority to be the Messiah's mom. Mary answered the angel who told her what God was asking her to do, "I'm the Lord's maid, ready to serve. Let it be with me just as you say" (Luke 1:38 MSG).

Esther, Joshua, and Mary did things no one else had ever done. There was no track record of success. Nothing in this world pointed to the work God invited them into, but God had special plans for them and gave them the authority to carry them out. He crowned them with glory and honor. And that same God who lived in Mary's womb for forty weeks has placed His Spirit inside our bodies. That same power that knocked down those Jericho walls and stopped a genocide in its tracks is available to us 24/7. Just like God had plans for Esther, Joshua, and Mary, He has plans for you and me.

If Jesus asks you to write a song and you get to sing it to the Lord and let Him know how much you love Him and remind yourself how much He loves you—who cares who else hears? That is a song worth writing.

If God nudges you to start an initiative providing healthy meals to underprivileged kids and it takes off slowly but supplies eight children with nutritious lunches daily, then look how you're impacting God's kingdom!

If God suggests you create gorgeous handmade greeting cards and you send them to friends and family on their birthdays and they are over-the-top touched by the beauty and creativity and feel seen and special, then what does it matter if your Etsy sales are low?

If you don't write that song, start that initiative, or craft those cards, who will?

You don't have to be famous or rich or connected. You are a citizen of heaven, crowned with glory. God has made you a ruler over the works of His hands. When you do this work for Him, it will be blessed. Maybe not in the way you imagine but in beautiful ways God has prepared. Whatever God calls you to, He gives you the authority to do it.

Sounds like it's time to stop making excuses, shut out the lies of the enemy, and start exercising our authority.

—— RESTORE ——

What do you hear God calling you to that maybe you're hesitant to step into?

What's stopping you?

What tool do you have that could help you act on God's call (your laptop, guitar, oven, classroom, etc.)? Post these two verses on that tool, substituting "me" for "them":

You crowned me with glory and honor.
    You made me a ruler over the works of
        your hands;
you put everything under my feet.

LORD, our Lord,
    How majestic is your name in all the earth!
        (based on Psalm 8:5–6, 9)

3

TWO TRUTHS AND A LIE

Psalm 12

Help, LORD, for no one is faithful anymore;
those who are loyal have vanished from
the human race.
Everyone lies to their neighbor;
they flatter with their lips
but harbor deception in their hearts.

May the LORD silence all flattering lips
and every boastful tongue—
those who say,
"By our tongues we will prevail;
our own lips will defend us—who is lord
over us?"

"Because the poor are plundered and the
needy groan,
I will now arise," says the LORD.
"I will protect them from those who
malign them."
And the words of the LORD are flawless,
like silver purified in a crucible,
like gold refined seven times.

You, LORD, will keep the needy safe
and will protect us forever from the wicked,
who freely strut about
when what is vile is honored by the human
race.

Have you ever played two truths and a lie? Someone in a group makes three statements. I could say, "I'm a mom of four. I play guitar. And I've pierced at least ten people's ears."

The group has to guess which statement is the lie. Then I'd confess, "Actually I don't play guitar. But I wish I did."

We'd chat about my friends in college who asked me to pierce their ears, and it would evolve into other people's stories of guitar playing, kids, and ear piercing. It's a fun icebreaker to help a class, team, or small group get to know one another. But that's because the lie is revealed quickly. It's just part of the game, not meant to deceive anyone.

When I leased shopping malls for a living, there were plenty of lies scattered throughout conversations, but no one stood up at the end of a meeting and disclosed the lies. It became tricky to know who or what I could trust.

My job was to negotiate with stores like Bath & Body Works and Old Navy to open in my company's malls and pay us rent. If you've ever rented an apartment you get the gist. We were the landlord. The stores were the tenants. The difference is that there is typically a specific rent for a two-bedroom apartment in a complex—no matter who you are or how much your salary is. In a shopping mall, square footage, location within the mall, and projected sales are all variables in determining the rent. The owner of the mall wants the best stores in their properties. Lululemon and The Lego Store draw more customers and higher sales, and in turn more retailers who are willing to pay higher rents. The shops, of course, want the best locations and the lowest rents.

Here's where the two truths and a lie came into play. Coworkers would, as they called it, "puff" the sales of the stores in a mall to lure in new retailers and convince them they could pay more rent. I also sat across the table from retailers who would round down how much they were paying in other malls in order to negotiate lower rent packages. I'm not saying everyone was dishonest. But usually there was some sort of fabrication—that lie mixed in with the truth.

I recall one retailer saying to me after I shared some sales figures, "Sure, but we all know you're exaggerating."

But I wasn't.

I was telling the truth.

This guy laughed and shook his head when I told him so. Not because he didn't trust me specifically but because that's not how the game was played. It was standard in the industry for both sides to tell a lie or two, so much so that nobody believed anyone else.

I adore fashion and travel and learning new things, and I got to be immersed in all of that as part of my position. But the pressure to paint a prettier picture than was there wore on me. Sometimes I slipped and caved to that pressure. The Ten Commandments clearly state that we shouldn't lie, but being honest was hurting my deals. However, if I joined in the game, I felt awful, as I should. I wanted to cry out like King David, the author of Psalm 12, "Help, LORD, for no one is faithful anymore" (vv. 1–2). Everyone seemed to "harbor deception in their hearts."

There were certainly honest people in the industry. My regional team was full of incredible folks I adored. But some days it felt like everyone was lying and flattering and boasting and no one was fully trustworthy or dependable or, to use the psalmist's word, "faithful." It felt like the last line of Psalm 12, that "what is vile is honored by the human race." If you lied well, convinced the person sitting across from you that your mall or store was better than it actually was, you were rewarded with a better deal and a bigger bonus check. It was a dangerous place to sit.

Do you have any spheres of life where it feels like that? Where everyone tells little white lies? Where bending the truth seems to be the currency to get ahead? It could be a group of parents on the sidelines. Somehow meals and grocery shopping come up and everyone shares their homemade organic recipes (which they cannot *all* be making *all* the time). You'd been planning to swing through the Chipotle drive-through on the way home, but when someone asks what you're making for dinner you start to doubt yourself. And you mutter something like, "I was thinking of making a big salad."

You didn't say you were actually going to make that salad—just thinking about it, right? And in the midst of a conversation laced with lies (you know for a fact their child eats candy bars), you feel like less of a parent than you felt an hour ago and possibly even cornered into manipulating the truth just a tad—or maybe more.

Maybe it's at a conference where everyone brags about the wonderful work they've accomplished, the contacts they have, and the new secret project they're working on, and you feel inferior and inclined to maybe, just maybe, exaggerate some of your successes so no one will think less of you. Perhaps it's at the gym and folks are chatting up how many miles they usually run or how often they typically lift. When asked, you feel like you need to make your workouts sound more intense or frequent than they are in reality.

When everyone around us is puffing the truth, it can be both hurtful and contagious. It's hard not to compare, to be fully confident in who we are and how we're approaching things. But Psalm 12 reminds us of who our God is, what He does for us, and how and why we should stick with the truths and eliminate the lies.

Who is our God?

Verse 6 says His words are flawless, like purified silver, like refined gold.

Such sweet relief there! We never have to guess whether God is telling the truth or not. He always is. Not only does He tell the truth; He *is* the truth. Jesus tells us in John 14:6, "I am the way and the truth and the life." And again, in John 18:37 (NLT), "Actually, I was born and came into the world to testify to the truth. All who love the truth recognize that what I say is true."

I do love the truth.

I want other people to tell me the truth. I want to know how they feel and where they stand. I want to know where my kids were and what happened there. If my husband had something wonky happen at work or got a call from a frazzled family member that's stressing him out, I want him to tell me so I can help if possible. I don't want him to say, "I'm fine," and then seem distant, leaving me to guess what's wrong.

One of my best friends and I have a running joke about what we "made" for dinner. We text each other pictures of to-go bags, pizza boxes, and rotisserie chickens, because we're both juggling family and writing and some days that means we don't have time to cook. But we'll also share if we made something yummy, because that feels good too. There is such relief in the honesty between us, because it gives me the freedom to prepare a delicious homemade meal when I can *and* to order out when I can't, and in both to feel fully confident that I'm doing the work God has called me to do.

I want the people around me to tell the truth, because then it's easier for me to confess that I haven't been working out, but I'm here at the gym today and hoping to make it a new habit. Or that I haven't a clue how to make my yard look gorgeous. Does anyone have tips for easy-to-plant flowers with minimum maintenance?

As Christians, we're called to live and love like Jesus. Meaning, since He's honest, we should also aim to be honest. When we put down our defenses and share our true selves, there's less need for bragging all around. And even when that isn't so easy, or when everyone else is inflating their realities and the only way to keep up seems to be to do the same, Psalm 12 reminds us that we don't need to keep up:

> You, LORD, will keep the needy safe
> and will protect us forever from the
> wicked,
> who freely strut about
> when what is vile is honored by the human
> race. (vv. 7–8)

I hope you didn't skip over that.

The Lord will keep us safe. He will protect us.

That doesn't mean it will always be easy to avoid the dishonesty game. We're human. We live in a world where lies abound, or as the psalmist says, where "everyone lies to their neighbor" (v. 2). Advertisers lie about how easy things will be if we purchase their product. Social media lies by showing us only the highlights of others' lives. Friends and family lie in attempts to protect themselves or sometimes us. I kick myself for times I've stretched or bent the truth because in the moment it felt safer or easier. In the end, it wasn't.

But Jesus is the truth. And the Lord will keep us safe. So there is no reason to jump on the exaggeration train with the "vile" and "wicked" described in Psalm 12. Instead, we can tell the truth. We can stand proudly in who we are, because God created us in His image (Genesis 1:27). We can own up to our mistakes, because that's the way to learn from them and to repair any damage that might have been done. We can share where we're weak, because God's power is made perfect in our weakness (2 Corinthians 12:9). Whether you've been lied to or want to work on being more fully honest, or both, the Lord will protect you forever.

This could look different for all of us. God protecting us from lies could look like God pairing you with a wonderful counselor who helps you heal from past lies. This could mean God offering you ways out when you're put in a situation that triggers deceitful behavior (1 Corinthians 10:13). Maybe it means coming clean about something you lied about and God offering you overwhelming peace. Perhaps God will put someone in your life who reminds you of Christ's truth to help you stomp out the lies you've been telling yourself. Jesus fights for the truth—in our world and in our hearts.

Our Savior was absolute Truth hanging on a cross between two criminals at Calvary. He wasn't there to condemn those men. Nope. That's never Christ's intent. His goal is to love the world—including you and me, no matter how honest or dishonest we've been. No matter how hard some areas of our lives may feel when we've been deluged in dishonesty. In intense pain and agony, Jesus forgave the criminal who confessed his sin and recognized Jesus as innocent. To this man Jesus said, "Today you will be with me in paradise" (Luke 23:43).

Jesus inverted the game. His goal is not to come up with the most convincing lie, but instead Christ offers the most remarkable truth. The truth that He died on that cross to give us eternal, rich, full, abundant life. That He sees us in both the pain of the lies we've been told and the shame of the lies we've uttered and loves us just the same. That He will never ever forsake us. If there was hope for that criminal next to Jesus on the cross, there's hope for all of us. You and me. The Lord will protect us forever from the wicked.

1. The Lord will protect us.
2. Forever.

Those are two truths that will never lie.

──────────── RESTORE ────────────

Is there a sphere of life where you're tempted to bend the truth?

Is there a lie you've been told that is hard to heal from?

Take a few minutes to either journal or pray about it. That's what King David did. He was frustrated by the deceit around him and how it affected him, so he wrote a song to God about it. God wants to hear everything from us—including how we're in a place that tempts us to lie, makes us question the truth, or deceives us. Take it to Him today and let Him reassure you of His protection.

4

TEARS AND TISSUES

Psalm 13

*How long, LORD? Will you forget me
        forever?
    How long will you hide your face from
        me?
How long must I wrestle with my thoughts
    and day after day have sorrow in my
        heart?
    How long will my enemy triumph over
        me?*

*Look on me and answer, LORD my God.
    Give light to my eyes, or I will sleep in
        death,
and my enemy will say, "I have overcome
        him,"
    and my foes will rejoice when I fall.*

*But I trust in your unfailing love;
    my heart rejoices in your salvation.
I will sing the LORD's praise,
    for he has been good to me.*

My mother-in-law is always searching for some-thing—her purse, her phone, her keys. But as she looks around with a confused expression in her pale blue eyes, the truth is that what she's actually searching for is her memory.

She has Alzheimer's. And it's a horrible thing to watch. The blank look on her face when we mention someone she loves but their name no longer holds meaning to her. The terrifying split second when she trips, tumbling toward the sidewalk, because she forgot that you lift your feet up when there's a step. The awkward moment in the ladies' room when I hear her fumbling at her door latch because she doesn't recall how to open it or when we get to the sink and she taps the faucet with her index finger because she doesn't remember that knobs turn. It's absolutely heartbreaking.

We love her. And we try to do what we can. She's in a wonderful care facility with kind, attentive helpers, a café that rivals local bistros, and bright, modern rooms. We visit often and take her for walks or out for ice cream, telling her we love her and getting her to giggle. And we pray. Oh, how we pray. I pray. My husband prays. Our kids pray. We ask our small groups and friends to join us in prayer for her. My husband's siblings and their families are also lifting up prayers. We pray for her peace and her joy. That she knows God loves her, that we love her. But we also pray for a miracle. That a scientist discovers a cure for Alzheimer's. That her brain stops short-circuiting and starts functioning normally again.

But after years of countless prayers, she keeps getting worse. And it keeps getting harder.

I hear King David's plea in my mind:

> How long, LORD? Will you forget me
>   forever?
> How long will you hide your face from
>   me?
> How long must I wrestle with my thoughts

and day after day have sorrow in my
    heart?
How long will my enemy triumph over
    me? (Psalm 13:1–2)

I know God hears our prayers. I know God wants
what's best for all of us. I believe He loves my mother-
in-law, Diane, that He sees her and weeps. I believe what
Paul wrote to the Romans, "And we know that in all
things God works for the good of those who love him,
who have been called according to his purpose" (8:28).

But from where I sit, I can't see the good in this situation. My brain can't even predict something good that
could come from it. It's sad. It's hard. For Diane. For her
family. Where is the good here, God?

Look on me and answer, LORD my God.
    Give light to my eyes, or I will sleep in
        death,
and my enemy will say, "I have overcome
    him,"
    and my foes will rejoice when I fall. (Psalm
        13:3–4)

Psalms like this are important. They take our pain, our
concerns, our doubts and give them language. They give
us permission to come to God with our disappointment
and anger. But they also give us hope. Pastor and author
John Mark Comer explains it like this: "The psalms we
read in the dark night are the ones that don't resolve.
They don't end with, *Things were really bad, but it all
worked out.* They end with, *God, things are really bad,
and I don't see your hand at work, but I trust you.*"[3]

Are we trusting God in the struggles?

I wrestle like the psalmist. I beg God to reveal what
He's doing. I repeat, "Look on me and answer, LORD my
God. Give light to my eyes" (v. 3).

I wonder how Alzheimer's can be "good." I want to trust, but that's so hard. I still experience pain every time I see my mother-in-law. When she fumbles with silverware, no longer remembering how to use it. When she asks the same question she's already asked several times. I want to cry until all the tears amount to something— that somehow this heap of soggy tissues can be magically transformed into a box of memories. And I go back to Romans 8:28. Again. *All things, God?* I'm ready for the good. But instead of showing me how this could possibly work for good, God turns my eyes to the preceding verses:

> We know that the whole creation has been groaning as in the pains of childbirth right up to the present time. Not only so, but we ourselves, who have the firstfruits of the Spirit, groan inwardly as we wait eagerly for our adoption to sonship, the redemption of our bodies. For in this hope we were saved. But hope that is seen is no hope at all. Who hopes for what they already have? But if we hope for what we do not yet have, we wait for it patiently. (vv. 22–25)

Ahhhh. Hope. It's what I want and what I crave.

So I pray through these verses in Romans in search of it: *God, everything about Alzheimer's makes me groan! You realize this, Lord. We are waiting for the redemption of our bodies. And for the healing of Diane's mind. We will cling to hope. Even when it's hard to see. I will wait, Lord. I don't know how long. But I will wait. Because you are my joy and my hope.*

So, like John Mark Comer and Paul, I cling to the intangible hope—the hope the author of Hebrews instructs us to cling to when he says, "Let us hold unswervingly to the hope we profess, for he who promised is faithful" (10:23).

Even though I'm asking God (just like David did when he wrote this psalm), "How long, LORD? . . . How long will I wrestle with my thoughts?" (vv. 1–2), "How long will Diane wrestle with her tangled thoughts?" I still cling to God's faithfulness.

And it gives me hope.

Is there something groaning in your life? Something that feels impossible? Something where you struggle to see how God could possibly use it for good? Is there something you've been praying for on repeat that fills your heart with sorrow or pain? Have you lost hope? Or do you still have a glimmer? Grab hold of it as tight as you can!

Paul reminds us to hope in things we can't see. That's not easy. Especially on days when the fear and pain feel like too much. But it is possible.

I can't see the wind, but I still believe in it. I still trust that when it blows it can make leaves tumble or trees sway. And even though love has no outline or shape, I believe in and have fully experienced it. I trust that my kids love me, even when I don't see them all day long, even if we have a disagreement. So it is possible to believe in things we can't see or touch. Hoping and trusting are still the right things to do. And the good news? We don't have to do them on our own.

Paul continues, "In the same way, the Spirit helps us in our weakness. We do not know what we ought to pray for, but the Spirit himself intercedes for us through wordless groans. And he who searches our hearts knows the mind of the Spirit, because the Spirit intercedes for God's people in accordance with the will of God" (Romans 8:26–27).

Sigh. The Holy Spirit is interceding for us. When we don't know what to pray for, when we've run out of words, the Spirit steps in. How beautiful is that? God knows that from our earthly perspective we can't see everything He's doing, can't fathom how any of this will ever turn to good. But God also knows that we're only seeing through a crack in the door and that when the door swings open we'll get a gorgeous view of so much more, of the bigger picture, of how God *has* been working things together for our good, for the good of our loved ones, for the good of His people.

So (1) we're not alone.

And (2) we've seen God move before. I have. I bet you have too. Maybe you didn't think of it that way. But at some point you've seen a sick loved one get well, a heartbroken friend find love, a door open that felt like it had been slammed shut, or a broken heart healed. You might have seen a friend who went through detox eventually help others through a recovery program or witnessed a family member struggling with loneliness open their home to someone who couldn't afford an apartment, giving them both companionship and lower expenses. God protected them.

Maybe you haven't just witnessed these miracles, but experienced them firsthand. God promises to be faithful. If we stop to sort through our memories, we've all seen Him be faithful before. We've seen God use bad things and flip them into situations way better than we could have dreamed up. God is working even when we can't see it.

We can cling to God's goodness and faithfulness. We can be hopeful for when He'll move again. The prophet Isaiah reassures us, "Those who hope in the LORD will renew their strength. They will soar on wings like eagles; they will run and not grow weary, they will walk and not be faint" (40:31).

Are you ready to soar and run and have your strength renewed? Hope in the Lord. And because we have hope, while we wait and cry and flail, we can join with King David, who in the midst of his trial praised God:

41

But I trust in your unfailing love;
   my heart rejoices in your salvation.
I will sing the LORD's praise,
   for he has been good to me. (Psalm
    13:5–6)

Amen.

RESTORE

Do you have any prayers that haven't been answered?

List three ways God has been faithful to you in the past.

Write God a thank-you note. Thank Him for the ways He's been there for you. Include in the note either this direct quote from the psalm above or your own interpretation of it: "My heart rejoices in your salvation. I will sing the LORD's praise, for he has been good to me" (vv. 5–6).

Then ask God to flood you with hope.

5

SAFETY IN A SQUALL

Psalm 16

Keep me safe, my God,
for in you I take refuge.

I say to the LORD, *"You are my Lord;*
apart from you I have no good thing."
I say of the holy people who are in the land,
"They are the noble ones in whom is all
my delight."
Those who run after other gods will suffer
more and more.
I will not pour out libations of blood to
such gods
or take up their names on my lips.

LORD, *you alone are my portion and my cup;*
you make my lot secure.
The boundary lines have fallen for me in
pleasant places;
surely I have a delightful inheritance.
I will praise the LORD, *who counsels me;*
even at night my heart instructs me.
I keep my eyes always on the LORD.
With him at my right hand, I will not be
shaken.

Therefore my heart is glad and my tongue
rejoices;
my body also will rest secure,

because you will not abandon me to the
realm of the dead,
nor will you let your faithful one see decay.
You make known to me the path of life;
you will fill me with joy in your presence,
with eternal pleasures at your right hand.

My chest feels tight. Sitting still makes me jittery, like I'll pop out of my skin, so I have to stand and pace. My thoughts are racing so quickly I can't even articulate what they are—no words, just ideas, worries, angst, fear.

This is a pretty raw peek into my frantic headspace when I'm faced with a reoccurring issue in my life that triggers fear and irrational thinking.

Sometimes I can deal with it, blow it off. Sometimes my defense mechanism of sarcasm kicks in, and I say something snarky as a means to protect myself from these hard emotions. Of course, then I immediately feel guilty for saying something unkind. If I'm in a room with other people when this happens, I walk out, go to the bathroom, get a drink of water, anything to distract myself. It's a Psychology 101 reaction. When we feel like we're in danger, we respond with fight or flight—meaning we either kick and scream and attack or run away. If someone I love is in danger, I'll fight for them. Every time. But if I'm the one who feels threatened, I choose the latter—flight.

In these moments a single thought repeats against the din of my internal alarms clanging and reminds me that God is my calming force. I need to intentionally seek Him, and I need to do it pronto.

God, I need you.

Reading Psalm 16 can be the perfect prescription for me in this scenario. Its words give me something to focus on, to take me away from troubling memories of the past and concerning what-ifs in the future. When I can't even put my emotions into words, the opening lines of this psalm are my heart's cry:

> Keep me safe, my God,
> for in you I take refuge. (v. 1)

It's as if King David, the author of this song, knew how I feel. Because this is exactly what I need right now. Safety. Refuge. Please, God.

I keep reading and the words are the words I would speak on my own if my brain was rational, but it's not. I'm frightened, like hands-balled-in-fists-stomach-clenched-eyes-bugged-out frightened. But I'm sitting in my family room. I *know* that I am actually safe. My family is safe. But still, past trauma makes me *feel* vulnerable, unprotected. The lines of this psalm remind me of what is true.

> I say to the LORD, "You are my Lord;
> apart from you I have no good thing."
> (v. 2)

My breathing becomes less shallow, more normal. The thoughts that terrify me feel less oppressive. God feels so much closer. It's not that I've been able to process and dismiss my fears one by one; it's just that I'm reminded that God is good. And He is my Savior. And those two truths ground and center me. I get through a few more verses, slowing my pulse.

> LORD, you alone are my portion and my cup;
> you make my lot secure. (v. 5)

Yes, Jesus, you are what I need. You keep me secure when I feel unstable. You are like a flagpole holding me in place when I flap wildly in the wind. And at the same time, you calm the wind itself, allowing me to exhale, stop flailing, and be still. Which makes sense. This isn't the first or last time you've calmed the winds.

The gospel writer Luke tells of it:

> A squall came down on the lake, so that the boat was being swamped, and they were in great danger.
>
> The disciples went and woke [Jesus], saying, "Master, Master, we're going to drown!"
>
> He got up and rebuked the wind and the raging waters; the storm subsided, and all was calm. (8:23–24)

That storm subsided.

My mental storm is subsiding too. That doesn't mean there won't be more storms. This will happen again. I mean, I'm in a boat, and storms will come my way out here. But Jesus can calm all of them.

You, Jesus, have the power to calm raging waters and keep me from drowning. This thing that has my stomach in knots has no power over you, Jesus. None. When the winds start blowing again, you'll calm those waves of fear. I can trust in you. And now that I feel this storm settling, Lord, as I feel your safe arms around me, I see that the fear was unnecessary. You keep me safe. You always do.

When I read in Psalm 16:6 that "the boundary lines have fallen for me in pleasant places," I'm reminded that here within God's boundary lines—in the places that God has planned for me and you—the life He promises us is pleasant. His grace is lavish.

I don't ever want to jump out of the boat into the storm without you, God. Here with you? It's delightful.

So I will do as King David did as he wrote this song to you, God: "I keep my eyes always on the LORD. With him at my right hand, I will not be shaken" (v. 8).

I feel this, Father. I feel you here beside me. You guard

all that is mine (v. 5). I won't be shaken. Because I have you to keep me safe. Because you keep me strong.

> Therefore my heart is glad and my tongue
> rejoices;
> my body also will rest secure. (v. 9)

The thing that happens—that makes me anxious—is out of my control. But when I let Him, our good and gracious God gives me a way out of the fear and into peace.

He offers this to you too. God can be your portion and your cup. He wants to put you in pleasant places. Even if you don't know Him or trust Him, Jesus offers this to you. Will you accept? He wants to calm your storms and keep you secure. He has the power to quiet a squall—both the kind that rages on the surface of a sea and the kind that wreaks havoc on our hearts. Even when the cold, salty waves sting our eyes and the tossing boat knocks us off our feet, Jesus says to whatever is attacking us, "Be still!"

And if we look at Him, the One whose love never ends, then we can regain our footing, see more clearly, and breathe in and out again without fear of gulping mouthfuls of briny water. We can find the peace and strength in Jesus that we need to continue.

I don't know what your storms are, which things cause your thoughts to spiral, your palms to sweat, your heart to beat too fast, your instincts to either lash out or retreat. But I do know whatever they are and whenever they happen, our faithful, loving God can keep you safe. All you have to do is call out His name—Jesus.

RESTORE

Do you have a reoccurring storm in your life? A situation or person who puts you into fight-or-flight mode? That makes you angry or frightened? That makes you lose your self-control?

Just thinking of this situation may be triggering for you. Don't dwell on the hows and whys of the culprit. Instead, dwell on Jesus. He is always with you. He will keep you safe. Direct your thoughts to Psalm 16. Read the whole thing out loud.

Was there a stanza that resonated with you? If so, write it out. If you sense that you may face this threat again in the future, put the words of this psalm somewhere you can access them quickly at that time.

6

SUNSET WALKS

Psalm 19

The heavens declare the glory of God;
 the skies proclaim the work of his hands.
Day after day they pour forth speech;
 night after night they reveal knowledge.
They have no speech, they use no words;
 no sound is heard from them.
Yet their voice goes out into all the earth,
 their words to the ends of the world.
In the heavens God has pitched a tent for the
  sun.
 It is like a bridegroom coming out of his
  chamber,
 like a champion rejoicing to run his course.
It rises at one end of the heavens
 and makes its circuit to the other;
 nothing is deprived of its warmth.

The law of the LORD is perfect,
 refreshing the soul.
The statutes of the LORD are trustworthy,
 making wise the simple.
The precepts of the LORD are right,
 giving joy to the heart.
The commands of the LORD are radiant,
 giving light to the eyes.
The fear of the LORD is pure,
 enduring forever.

*The decrees of the L*ORD *are firm,*
    and all of them are righteous.

They are more precious than gold,
    than much pure gold;
they are sweeter than honey,
    than honey from the honeycomb.
By them your servant is warned;
    in keeping them there is great reward.
But who can discern their own errors?
    Forgive my hidden faults.
Keep your servant also from willful sins;
    may they not rule over me.
Then I will be blameless,
    innocent of great transgression.

May these words of my mouth and this medi-
        tation of my heart
    be pleasing in your sight,
    L*ORD, my Rock and my Redeemer.*

After dinner in the summer, chatter spills over from our kitchen onto our cul-de-sac as our family heads out for a sunset walk. It feels good to move a bit after a meal and to breathe in the warm summer air, thick with humidity and sweet with honeysuckle. And although we've never truly set a goal for these strolls, we do call them "sunset walks." As we're unwinding from our days and unplugging from everything digital, a couple of us usually still bring phones, because the evening sky in our neighborhood is almost always spectacular and we're hoping to capture it in a picture. I don't know if it's because of how our subdivision is situated or because we live in a small college town away from pollution and tall buildings (well, actually a mile outside of a small college town in a neighborhood across from a rather large cornfield), but the view of the sky is splendid—deep tangerine and fuchsia swirled with plum and dipped in gold. Sometimes the clouds are like cotton candy, so thick and fluffy you want to cozy up in them. Some evenings they're thin wisps giving the sun's glow an appearance of melted wax. Every night it causes me to pause, to find stillness within, to ponder God's goodness, to marvel at His creativity and kindness to make something so intensely beautiful, knowing full well it will only last a moment, but still He finds it a worthwhile endeavor.

I walk with my family and our conversation hushes as we all gaze at the sky. I wonder how anyone could see this majesty and doubt God's existence. Even the sky shouts of His glory.

King David describes the sun's magnificence in Psalm 19:4–6.

> In the heavens God has pitched a tent for the
>   sun.
>   It is like a bridegroom coming out of his
>   chamber,
>   like a champion rejoicing to run his course.
> It rises at one end of the heavens
>   and makes its circuit to the other;
>   nothing is deprived of its warmth.

We can understand God better by reading the Bible. Sometimes we get a clearer idea of Him by listening to a sermon or attending a Bible study. Prayer is another wonderful way to know, feel, and comprehend God on a deep level. But taking in His artistry is another way to expand our picture of who God is.

We're bombarded with sounds all day long—music, livestreams, podcasts, shows. Words cram themselves into our heads from texts, emails, messages, articles, blogs, and books. As the Grinch laments in Dr. Seuss's classic, "And then! Oh, the noise! Oh, the Noise! Noise!

Noise! Noise! That's one thing he hated! The NOISE! NOISE! NOISE! NOISE!"⁴ Just typing this I picture that green Grinch holding his hands to his ears. It's strange, because we choose this noise, we turn it on, stuff our earbuds in our ears, and yet . . .

Sometimes the best way to get a breakthrough is not with words.

I know. I'm a writer and a word lover, but it's true. Moments of clarity are rarely found with noise, but with silence and beauty. The "speech without words" (see vv. 2–3) that a sunset delivers packs a powerful punch.

It is in this quiet loveliness that God speaks a thousand truths to my soul. It is as Madeleine L'Engle says in *Walking on Water*, "There is time in which to be, simply to be, that time in which God quietly tells us who we are and who he wants us to be. It is then that God can take our emptiness and fill it up with what he wants and drain away the business with which we inevitably get involved in the dailiness of human living."⁵

I feel and hear that as I gaze at the sun sinking lower in the sky, as the warm summer breeze blows my hair across my shoulders. I'm reminded of Christ's pure love for me. That this love prevails over anyone else's opinion, over anything that has happened to me on that day or any other. My worries drip off. I am filled with warmth and peace and joy. God speaks to me through this sunset as "the heavens declare the glory of God; the skies proclaim the work of his hands" (v. 1).

> Day after day [the heavens] pour forth speech;
>   night after night they reveal knowledge.
> They have no speech, they use no words;
>   no sound is heard from them.
> Yet their voice goes out into all the earth,
>   their words to the ends of the world.
>   (vv. 2–4)

No wonder my family ranging from ages fifteen to fifty-two, all dealing with their own personal struggles and triumphs, are also drawn to the magnetism of what we can find, of how we can hear God, if we take a moment to gaze at something He created. It is not in the sunset itself but in the One powerful and beautiful enough to dream up the sunset and bring it to life that my family finds refreshment for our souls.

I can have a similar experience sitting on our screened porch during a thunderstorm—lightning flashing in the distance, rain rhythmically pounding on the roof. I can smell the tinny scent of rain mixed with the rich, earthy smell of the ground it soaks. A tremor runs through my body when thunder booms. Yet on that porch I am safe and dry. There, God reminds me of both how powerful He is and how He protects me. And again without words, but by observing the heavens God created, my soul is cleansed.

The very first verse of the Bible points us to the sky: "In the beginning God created the heavens and the earth" (Genesis 1:1). The next thing God does is separate light from darkness, the exact thing a sunset or sunrise or thunderstorm does—showing us the distinction between night and day, dark and bright. God knows the difference and calls the light "good" (v. 4). I believe our souls also feel the difference.

Since these are the opening lines of our holy Scripture, shouldn't we take note?

So many things pull for our attention on any given day—toddlers with thousands of questions, aches in our bodies, bills that need to be paid, calls that need to be made, errands that need to be run. And these are important things. But in the midst of all the things, it's therapeutic for our souls to take time to gaze in wonder at the "glory of God . . . the work of his hands" (Psalm 19:1).

When I do, the day-to day struggles of living in this

world feel lighter. Instead of everything that's going on in my life bumping around in my brain, my to-dos and dreams and duties seem to sort into files of what matters most when I stare at the sky. And nothing feels too big or overwhelming, because did you see the way the purple weaves through the aqua on the side of that cloud?

Instead of my usual thinking through what I need to get done—move the chicken from the freezer to the fridge to thaw for tomorrow's dinner of quesadillas, oh and call the allergist to set up an appointment so we can get a refill on my daughter's EpiPen, so we can send it in to her school nurse who has gently and kindly emailed me twice—I just stand serenely, drinking in the color-saturated sky like a sponge.

I don't know what your day looks like, but whatever you do, wherever you live, take some time to gaze at the sky today. That might mean catching the sunrise on a morning jog or commute or stargazing from your front lawn or rooftop. But take a moment. Inhale. Exhale. The heavens declare the glory of God and the sky doesn't have a soul or a mouth. But we humans? We have been saved by His glory, loved by His glory, sustained by His glory (Hebrews 1:3). Shouldn't we declare it too? With our lips and in our hearts.

"May these words of my mouth and this meditation of my heart be pleasing in your sight, LORD, my Rock and my Redeemer" (Psalm 19:14). Amen.

———— RESTORE ————

When was the last time you gazed at the sky?

When in the next twenty-four hours can you make time to go on a sunset walk or a sunrise stroll or a stargazing expedition? Put it on your calendar. Perhaps invite a friend or family member to join you.

When you do this, allow yourself quiet and stillness to soak it all in. Afterward, journal your thoughts or discuss with someone special how it made you feel.

7

WHAT THOSE PRESENTS COST

Psalm 22

My God, my God, why have you forsaken me?
  Why are you so far from saving me,
  so far from my cries of anguish?
My God, I cry out by day, but you do not
    answer,
  by night, but I find no rest.

Yet you are enthroned as the Holy One;
  you are the one Israel praises.
In you our ancestors put their trust;
  they trusted and you delivered them.
To you they cried out and were saved;
  in you they trusted and were not put to
    shame.

But I am a worm and not a man,
  scorned by everyone, despised by the
    people.
All who see me mock me;
  they hurl insults, shaking their heads.
"He trusts in the LORD," *they say,*
  "let the LORD *rescue him.*
Let him deliver him,
  since he delights in him."

Yet you brought me out of the womb;
　　you made me trust in you, even at my
　　　　mother's breast.
From birth I was cast on you;
　　from my mother's womb you have been my
　　　　God.

Do not be far from me,
　　for trouble is near
　　and there is no one to help.

Many bulls surround me;
　　strong bulls of Bashan encircle me.
Roaring lions that tear their prey
　　open their mouths wide against me.
I am poured out like water,
　　and all my bones are out of joint.
My heart has turned to wax;
　　it has melted within me.
My mouth is dried up like a potsherd,
　　and my tongue sticks to the roof of my
　　　　mouth;
　　you lay me in the dust of death.

Dogs surround me,
　　a pack of villains encircles me;
　　they pierce my hands and my feet.
All my bones are on display;
　　people stare and gloat over me.
They divide my clothes among them
　　and cast lots for my garment.

But you, Lord, do not be far from me.
　　You are my strength; come quickly to help
　　　　me.
Deliver me from the sword,
　　my precious life from the power of the
　　　　dogs.
Rescue me from the mouth of the lions;
　　save me from the horns of the wild oxen.

I will declare your name to my people;
in the assembly I will praise you. (vv. 1–22)

I pulled the pale blue tissue paper from the brown bag printed with a shop's name I didn't recognize. Inside was a purse shaped like a barstool cushion flipped on its side—round and flat. It was a deep-green leather with suede fringe trimming the bottom. A strip of cowhide print accented the front, but instead of the standard brown spots they were a metallic green. It was hippie-chic and funky. I was in love.

When I talked to my brother later that day he said, "I know we don't normally buy each other things, but I saw that purse hanging on a rack and knew it belonged with you—not in that store. So I bought it."

The extravagance and fun of it all made me giggle like a teenager. The image of my brother walking through a boutique and pausing when he saw this little purse . . . was he with his daughter? His girlfriend? Just there by himself? And thinking of me, deciding to treat me? I felt loved.

The purse is great, but it isn't even in the same ballpark as the gifts Jesus gives us. Similar to how my brother knew this purse was perfect for my personality, Jesus knew His gifts would be perfect for us. And even though we didn't send Jesus any presents, He took a heap of them off the rack in heaven and sent them down to us, so we get to wear them each and every day. Jesus gives us freedom, forgiveness, abundant life, truth, peace, hope, light, and best of all love.

I want those things.

I need those things.

You?

I put unrealistic expectations on myself, so, yes, I need

freedom from thinking I need to do and be All. The. Things. I get grumpy and selfish and prideful, so I could really use some forgiveness. I walk around living on this earth and get bogged down with the everyday responsibilities and worries. But abundant life? One that is rich and fulfilling? Yes, please! I do want to know the truth. Because there are so many empty promises out there from everyone from pop stars to politicians, but I want the real truth. Jesus tells us himself that the truth will set us free (John 8:32).

My to-do lists are long. I experience daily confrontations, decisions that need to be made, friends and family in need. I feel pulled from this and that. Peace is a salve my soul craves.

On sad, desperate days I need hope. On scary, dark days I need light. And I don't know a person alive who doesn't want to be loved. Jesus gives us all this. Not as something we need to buy or earn but as a gift, because He thought of us and wanted us to have all these things.

But presents don't just appear. Yes, that purse was waiting for me in a box on my red brick doorstep, but my brother had to buy it, take it home, pack it up, address it, take it to the post office. The postal service scanned, loaded, and trucked my purse around on various routes until it made its way five hundred miles from my brother in Atlanta, Georgia, to me in Oxford, Ohio. Jesus also had to go through a process to get our gifts to us.

The analogy is rudimentary. What Jesus did for us is the ultimate sacrifice. Someone who sends us a surprise doesn't forfeit even a fraction of what Jesus surrendered for us. These things aren't on the same plane, but the gifts we give and receive do have a parallel to the gifts Jesus gives us, even though nothing, absolutely no gift, will ever equate to Jesus's gift of life.

My brother had to go to the post office. Jesus had to go somewhere infinitely more painful and complete—the cross. The purse cost my brother dollars. The gifts Jesus gives us cost Him His very life.

Psalm 22 tells us what this sacrifice entailed. In fact Jesus quoted this psalm from the cross: "About three in the afternoon Jesus cried out in a loud voice, *'Eli, Eli, lema sabachthani?'* (which means 'My God, my God, why have you forsaken me?')" (Matthew 27:46).

Which is verbatim what we find in Psalm 22:1: "My God, my God, why have you forsaken me?"

For years these last words of Jesus haunted me.

Did God the Father abandon Jesus that day? Did Jesus really believe the Father would forsake Him as Jesus sacrificed himself for God's children, for us?

And then I read Psalm 22. It's not one you usually see on T-shirts or stickers. It's never read as a closing prayer at church. It's painful, so we tend to steer clear of the words. But all the Jewish leaders who had made the case to have Jesus crucified would have known this psalm by heart. The Psalms were the prayer book of Jesus, the disciples, and all the rabbis, Pharisees, Sadducees, and chief priests. This was a prayer the Jewish people read and prayed and recited and memorized.

"My God, my God, why have you forsaken me?"

As soon as Jesus quoted the first verse of Psalm 22, all the Jews near the cross knew what came next:

> All who see me mock me;
> they hurl insults, shaking their heads. (v. 7)

Hadn't that just happened here in this place? The mocking? The insults?

> [The soldiers] stripped [Jesus] and put a scarlet robe on him, and then twisted together a crown of thorns and set it on his head. They put a staff in his right hand. Then they knelt in front of him and mocked him. "Hail, king

of the Jews!" they said. They spit on him, and took the staff and struck him on the head again and again. (Matthew 27:28–30)

And moments after that, the chief priests and teachers of the law literally spoke the words predicted in the psalm:

He trusts in God. Let God rescue him now if he wants him. (Matthew 27:43)

"He trusts in the LORD," they say,
"let the LORD rescue him." (Psalm 22:8)

Wild, isn't it?

How identical King David's words from centuries prior were to what was going on that Friday before Passover just outside the city walls of Jerusalem. That God knew exactly how things would go down. When Jesus spoke that first verse from Psalm 22, did the Jewish scholars and the crowd gasp? Did they start running through the psalm they'd prayed over and over again in their heads?

- "My mouth is dried up like a [broken piece of pottery], and my tongue sticks to the roof of my mouth" (Psalm 22:15). *Check.* "Later, knowing that everything had now been finished, and so that Scripture would be fulfilled, Jesus said, 'I am thirsty'" (John 19:28).
- "They pierce my hands and my feet" (Psalm 22:16). *Check.* That's how a crucifixion works. Nails in hands. Nails in feet.
- "A pack of villains encircles me" (Psalm 22:16). *Check.* Criminals were crucified on either side of Jesus. Also, the chief priests, the teachers of the law, and the elders all around the cross mocked Jesus while He was suffering inexplicable pain. Sounds like evildoings to me.

- "They divide my clothes among them and cast lots for my garment" (Psalm 22:18). *Check.* "When they had crucified him, they divided up his clothes by casting lots" (Matthew 27:35).

As the crowd watched what was going on, did they go through this same mental checklist? As we're going through it now, are we processing what it means?

Jesus was stripped, mocked, spit on, beaten repeatedly, and had nails driven through His feet and hands. In fact, those were the only things attaching our Lord to a large wooden cross. This is what He intentionally went through to secure His gift for us. Imagine trying to hold yourself up with your core strength so those nails wouldn't tear through your flesh. If you put your weight in your feet, it would be agonizing because there were nails there. If you tried to pull yourself up with your hands, that was also excruciating. And as unbearable as the pain was, crucifixion victims typically died of suffocation. The way they were positioned made it impossible to get enough oxygen for their lungs.

Jesus gave up His very breath for you and me. And He knew all along that's how it would go down. God even made sure it was written into the Scriptures hundreds of years ahead of time so people would know that had always been His plan. Jesus knew the humiliation and pain that was coming and chose it anyway.

Why? Why did He go through all that? Was it worth it? Jesus thought so.

Just like we might spend extravagantly to get someone we love an item that we know they need or that will make them smile. Just like we might go out of our way to the post office to mail a gift to someone we love. Just like we might give up some of our free time to purchase that gift, it's worth it. We want to do it. We can't wait for them to open it up.

And as much as we love the people in our lives, Jesus loves us so very much more. He created us. He has beautiful plans for us. He invites us to cultivate His kingdom with Him. And He gives us all the gifts we need to live out those plans, to step into the good work He has set out for us, to see ourselves as daughters and sons of the one true King (see 2 Corinthians 6:18).

Let's go over that list of gifts Jesus offers again—freedom, forgiveness, abundant life, truth, peace, hope, light, and best of all love.

They're all there for the taking. Wrapped up in beautiful packages waiting for us. The question is, Will we pull them out of their bags, rip off the decorated paper, and accept them?

The purse my brother got me is super snazzy but does me zero good if it sits on my closet floor. I have to slide my wallet, phone, and shiny pink lip gloss in it, slip my arm in the strap, and wear it. Which I promise is not an inconvenience but a privilege—an absolute treat.

The same is true with the gifts Jesus gives us. We have to accept them and use them if we want to experience the privilege and treat of having them.

Step into freedom.

Believe we're forgiven.

Reach out for abundant life.

Listen to truth.

Breathe in peace.

Choose hope over despair or worry.

Walk out of darkness and into light.

And allow our loving Savior to show us what real love looks like.

All gifts cost something—time, money, packing tape, or postage. But the gifts that Jesus gave us—they cost Him everything. That is perfect love. The kind He wants to shower on you right here. Right now.

—— RESTORE ——

What is a gift you've recently given? What did it cost you? Why did you incur that cost?

What's a gift you've recently received? How did it make you feel?

Write out the gifts listed in this chapter that Jesus offers: freedom, forgiveness, abundant life, truth, peace, hope, light, and best of all love. Spend some time in prayer thanking Jesus for these extravagant gifts and asking Him how you can fully accept each of them today.

8

SOUL RESTORATION

Psalm 23

The LORD is my shepherd, I lack nothing.
 He makes me lie down in green pastures,
he leads me beside quiet waters,
 he refreshes my soul.
He guides me along the right paths
 for his name's sake.
Even though I walk
 through the darkest valley,
I will fear no evil,
 for you are with me;
your rod and your staff,
 they comfort me.

You prepare a table before me
 in the presence of my enemies.
You anoint my head with oil;
 my cup overflows.
Surely your goodness and love will follow me
 all the days of my life,
and I will dwell in the house of the LORD
 forever.

In fifth grade Sunday school my teacher, Mr. Cook, challenged us to memorize the Twenty-Third Psalm. The prize? A bookmark with a picture of a lamb snuggled on a shepherd's lap and the psalm printed across the front. But as a people pleaser, the real prize for me would be if I could achieve this challenge for Mr. Cook by the following Sunday.

I read that psalm in my Bible morning and night that week. I pictured goodness and mercy following me around like Tinker Bell followed Peter Pan. I liked that image. I also liked the part about green pastures. My favorite hangout as a kid was the field behind our neighborhood where I rode bikes, climbed trees, and created adventures in my mind for hours on end. I can still smell the heavy, hypnotizing scent of Queen Anne's lace that permeated that field. That's what I thought of when I read about green pastures. And of course I wanted God to guide me there—it was my favorite place to be. The rest of the words sounded nice, and if I memorized them just right, I could make Mr. Cook proud.

I kept that bookmark.

Not because I won it, but because the words have continued to comfort me for decades. God has deepened my understanding of the everyday richness and fullness He offers. In fact, that prize from Mr. Cook no longer marks a page in my Bible but now lives under the pillow of one of my daughters. This psalm transcends generations.

Why? What does memorizing some pretty verses and a promise of goodness and mercy mean for me? For you? Today?

My typical morning looks like waking up, reading my Bible and journaling, getting breakfast ready for a family of six, exercising in some manner, then diving into my work until it's time to pick up my youngest from school. The afternoon routine of homework, meal prep, and getting people to practices, meetings, and rehearsals takes over. Our family ends up back in our house around 10 p.m., exhausted. But we still need to empty the trash, refill the paper towel holder, and replace the hand soap in the bathroom. Once those tasks are completed, I set the alarm for 5:45 a.m. Basically, I no longer spend hours riding my bike around a field and climbing trees. If I'm not intentional, I won't visit any green pastures—literal or figurative. I'll feel anything but still.

As Ferris Bueller said, "Life moves pretty fast. You don't stop and look around once in a while, you could miss it."[6]

Are we moving too fast? Are we missing it?

Because God provides green pastures.

God didn't intend for us to run around like chickens with our heads cut off. He wants us to see all the splendor. He wants to restore our souls. He leads us beside *still* waters, the psalm tells us.

Are we even seeking still waters?

We're all complaining about how busy we are, how stressed we are, how we're trying to keep all the balls in the air—but are we doing anything about it?

We have a remedy that many of us overlook or dismiss or don't seem to make time for, which is ironic. God offers rest to all of us. He wants it for us. It's called Sabbath. And He invented it from the beginning of the world: "By the seventh day God had finished the work he had been doing; so on the seventh day he rested from all his work. Then God blessed the seventh day and made it holy, because on it he rested from all the work of creating that he had done" (Genesis 2:2–3).

Ferris Bueller didn't invent the day off. God did. And He invites us to take advantage of it. God reminded Moses about this Sabbath when He handed him the Ten Commandments:

> Remember the Sabbath day by keeping it holy. Six days you shall labor and do all your work, but the seventh day is a sabbath to the LORD your God. On it you shall

not do any work, neither you, nor your son or daughter, nor your male or female servant, nor your animals, nor any foreigner residing in your towns. For in six days the LORD made the heavens and the earth, the sea, and all that is in them, but he rested on the seventh day. Therefore the LORD blessed the Sabbath day and made it holy. (Exodus 20:8–11)

God didn't create the Sabbath because He needed a rest. He's God. He doesn't get tired. God didn't tell us to take a day off every week because He didn't want us to get our work done. Like all of God's commands, this one is for our good. God instructs us to take one out of every seven days off so He can restore us. He made this day holy. He blessed this day. Why? Because God is our Good Shepherd, and He leads us to still waters. As the verses I memorized for Mr. Cook say,

> He *makes* me lie down in green pastures,
> he leads me beside quiet waters,
> he refreshes my soul. (Psalm 23:2–3,
> emphasis added)

Why does God have to *make* us lie down?

Because we're dumb sheep who, left to our own devices, either forget or refuse to do it ourselves.

Sabbath.

I knew that word back in Sunday school, but I never thought about what it meant to practice it. And, yes, Sabbath takes practice, but once you get the hang of it, it's like riding a bike in a field. Freeing. Peaceful. Restorative. Fun.

For decades my idea of Sabbath was going to church on Sundays. But that fourth commandment doesn't say, "Attend a worship service on your Sabbath." It reads, "Don't do any work." God loves it when we meet together to worship and learn about Him. And I'm pretty sure God grins when He sees His people gathering around the world on Sundays and reading the Bible and praying. But Sabbath is more than that. It's taking our to-dos, our work—whatever that is—and handing it over to God, saying, "I believe you are who you say you are. I believe that you are all-powerful and that you can get anything done—anything you need accomplished—whether or not I work today. I believe that when you ask me to take a break, it's for a good reason. I believe that you're able to keep the world spinning, my company running, my family fed, if that's your desire, even if I take a day off."

The LORD is my shepherd, I lack nothing.
(v. 1)

What actually defines *work*? What do you need to take a day off from?

That's between you and God.

For me, Sabbath means no writing, speaking, or Bible teaching work. This is tricky because I'm a Christian storyteller, so reading the Bible or listening to a sermon might give me some work ideas or help me clarify something I'm working on. I have to set up some pretty specific boundaries for myself. My email, social media, and work planner are off-limits on Sundays. I also intentionally do not pick up, say, C. S. Lewis's *Reflections on the Psalms* while writing this book on the Psalms. In fact, even if Lewis's book is sitting on my coffee table, I keep it closed and choose something else to read—a novel set in a lavender field in France perhaps. On my Sabbath if God gives me a clever idea for a new chapter or a fresh way to phrase something, I do *not* open my laptop but instead jot the idea on a sticky note, open the door to my writing nook (which I keep closed on Sundays), stick that note on my laptop, and quickly exit and shut the door. I don't ignore the idea, because I feel it's from God. I make the quick note and set it aside, trusting Him to help me pick it up on Monday.

For you this could look totally different.

One young mama in my Bible study considers cooking dinner her work. She has little kiddos, and the process drains her. So she cooks double on Saturdays and heats up leftovers on Sunday, freeing her from this labor. For me, cooking when I have time (versus frantically throwing together things in the kitchen in a time crunch) is luxurious. One Sunday my oldest daughter and I turned on Spotify to French café music—accordions accompanied by the brush of cymbals—and spent over two hours shredding sharp Gruyère, slicing thick chunks of baguette, and dancing around the kitchen preparing a fondue feast for our family. It was a blast, and nothing about it resembled work.

You know which things consume you maybe a bit too much.

If you're spinning so fast in your whirlwind that you don't know what you need a Sabbath from, stop right now. Ask God where you need to s-l-o-w down, what you need to hand over, what you should be taking a Sabbath from every seventh day.

Oh, and that. The seventh day. When God issued the original commandment, Saturday was the Sabbath. It still is for Jewish people around the world. For many Christians it's traditionally become Sunday, but it doesn't have to be. Talk to God about that too. What day makes the most sense for you to hand it all over to Him? What day can you turn off your phone or your alarm clock or your washer and dryer? There is one. I promise. God designed work, and He created us to be His coworkers (Genesis 2:15; 1 Corinthians 3:9). But He designed work to be completed in six days. Trust Him on this.

It's so hard to let go for an entire day. Especially of the things we're trying to control.

I hear you.

When I started practicing Sabbath, it was super challenging. I frequently picked up my phone by instinct. Someone emailed me—shouldn't I email them back? I didn't get much work accomplished on Thursday because of the field trip I chaperoned, so couldn't I sneak back some time now?

God doesn't want us to be legalistic about this. If you have a mandatory meeting for work on your scheduled Sabbath, He's totally cool with you flipping days that week. But God is smarter than us. And He sees right through our excuses. Be honest with Him. Not for God's sake. Remember, He doesn't need you to rest. You'll be the one to benefit from your Sabbath if you take one. This is for you. The Shepherd doesn't get anything out of His sheep sipping cool water and grazing on the greenest grass except happier sheep.

Get that? God wants goodness for us. One way He offers it to us is with Sabbath.

Jesus put it this way: "The Sabbath was made to meet the needs of people, and not people to meet the requirements of the Sabbath" (Mark 2:27 NLT).

God created the Sabbath for us! He made it so we would be fulfilled—so our needs of rest and restoration would be met. It's real. It works. This beautiful thing God designed for us when He created the universe actually restores our soul.

Sabbath has become my favorite day of the week.

Why? Because I exhale. I'm not rushing from church to the next thing and the next and the next. I take a slow sip of my mocha and savor the froth, let it tickle my tongue. I'm an introvert, so introverted things refuel my tank. I journal about the sermon we heard, or a song we sang, or a Bible passage we read at Sunday service. I call my mom or a friend and can be fully present for the conversation because I'm not trying to do anything else.

Sometimes I'll pull out my acrylics and paint, or maybe I'll write a couple of cards to friends. I'll go for a walk around campus with my kids or sit and read a book—and not just a snippet but an actual chapter or two or five if the day permits. I'll paint my fingernails and toes in candy-colored shades that make me smile.

When life dictates that my Sabbath has to be on the go, that's okay too. If one of my kids has an all-day soccer tournament out of town, we'll listen to a sermon in the car. I'll go for a walk or jog in the fresh air while my child warms up with their team. I might pop in earbuds and listen to an audiobook during halftime. I'll inhale and exhale. I will not open Instagram. I will not check my email. We'll pick up carryout on the way home.

By the end of the day I may be tired, but I'm not exhausted. I'm restored. My mind got to wander, not focus the whole time. I did some things I truly enjoy, that fill me up.

> You anoint my head with oil;
> my cup overflows. (Psalm 23:5)

If you're an extrovert, you'll refuel differently. Maybe visiting with friends over a bonfire in your backyard or a game night. You know the things that restore you.

Can you picture your green pasture now? For one of my friends, it's the woods by her grandma's house where she danced as a girl when no one was watching, uninhibited in the dappled sunlight. If you don't have one, what's the pasture you've always dreamed of lying down in?

I see my field, and at the far end the bending arms of the giant willow tree, its branches dangling like beaded curtains to hide behind, its trunk an inviting throne to lean against while I listen to the bees buzzing among the fragrant, lacy white flowers. I spot a bumpy toad bouncing along a dusty patch of ground. I close my eyes and let the wind whisper across my face.

Now picture your green pasture. Imagine the sound of your quiet water nearby—the trickle of a stream, the rush of waves, the silence of a pond. Linger there.

This is what God offers us with Sabbath. Peace. Restoration. It might take several weeks or months or iterations of practicing Sabbath, of really letting go of some things, of releasing yourself to the rest God intended when He created the Sabbath. It was never meant as something for you to check off your list or as something God would be angry about if you didn't do or didn't do "correctly." God's not evaluating you on how you take Sabbath; He's inviting you into it. It was always meant as a gift. Receive it. Relish it.

At my field in my mind, I stay. As long as I like. As long as I'm home by dinner. Then I pop on my bike that I leaned against the other side of the tree and pedal home in the warm summer air. I *bump bump* over twigs and ruts, my hair blowing back behind me as I ride. I am free. My soul is restored.

Yours can be too.

> Surely your goodness and love will follow me
>   all the days of my life,
> and I will dwell in the house of the LORD
>   forever. (v. 6)

See what happens if you try to take Sabbath, intentionally setting aside a day each week for God to nourish you. You can trust Him to lead you. It'll be way better than a bookmark or bragging rights. He promises to protect you from your enemies, to guide you, to comfort you. God promises His love will follow you all the days of your life. Not someday in the future but *all* the days. Will you let Him lead you? Will you allow your Good Shepherd to restore your soul?

───── RESTORE ─────

Do you currently practice Sabbath? If not, commit to starting this week. Pick a day. Choose something you define as work and intentionally lay it down for at least a couple of hours. If you already practice Sabbath, is there something you could do to make it richer, more freeing? Try it this week!

Take a five-minute "Sabbath" right now. Picture a place that soothes your soul—either one you've been to before or one that lives in your imagination. Spend a few minutes there. Allow yourself to unwind and reconnect to Christ's peace and love.

9

HAND-DRAWN MAP
OF PARIS

Psalm 25

In you, LORD my God,
  I put my trust.

I trust in you;
  do not let me be put to shame,
  nor let my enemies triumph over me.
No one who hopes in you
  will ever be put to shame,
but shame will come on those
  who are treacherous without cause.

Show me your ways, LORD,
  teach me your paths.
Guide me in your truth and teach me,
  for you are God my Savior,
  and my hope is in you all day long.
Remember, LORD, your great mercy and love,
  for they are from of old.
Do not remember the sins of my youth
  and my rebellious ways;
according to your love remember me,
  for you, LORD, are good.

Good and upright is the LORD;
  therefore he instructs sinners in his ways.
He guides the humble in what is right
  and teaches them his way.

All the ways of the LORD *are loving and
    faithful
    toward those who keep the demands of his
    covenant.
For the sake of your name,* LORD,
    forgive my iniquity, though it is great.

Who, then, are those who fear the LORD?
    *He will instruct them in the ways they
    should choose.
They will spend their days in prosperity,
    and their descendants will inherit the land.
The* LORD *confides in those who fear him;
    he makes his covenant known to them.
My eyes are ever on the* LORD,
    *for only he will release my feet from the
    snare.*

*Turn to me and be gracious to me,
    for I am lonely and afflicted.
Relieve the troubles of my heart
    and free me from my anguish.
Look on my affliction and my distress
    and take away all my sins.
See how numerous are my enemies
    and how fiercely they hate me!*

*Guard my life and rescue me;
    do not let me be put to shame,
    for I take refuge in you.
May integrity and uprightness protect me,
    because my hope,* LORD, *is in you.*

*Deliver Israel, O God,
    from all their troubles!*

The first time I went to Paris it's miraculous that I
even arrived, let alone that I got there safely. I was

twenty-one years old, studying in London for the summer, and had been selected by my program to go on a three-day research trip to Paris along with two of my classmates. None of us had ever left the United States before, and now we were leaving the country we were visiting to go to *another* country all by ourselves. One of our advisers helped us book cheap student airfare that allowed us to fly from London to Paris and back for forty-five dollars each—no lie. That would get us to France, but then what?

I was the only one in our group who spoke French, and let's be clear that meant Ohio high school classroom French. This was before cell phones, Tripadvisor, or Google. The only kind of maps that existed were on paper. Fortunately, one of the guys on our trip, Mark, had been to Paris before. He sat the three of us down, grabbed a piece of notebook paper and a pen, and explained what to do once we landed and where to stay. He wrote:

1. Train to Saint-Michel–Notre-Dame metro stop
2. Eat gyros in the Latin Quarter

And then he drew in blue ink a tiny map indicating the following things: a street with a doodle of a car on it, the Jardin du Luxembourg, and across the boulevard from the grand park a Naf Naf store on one corner and Hotel L'Europa across from it. That's where we were supposed to stay. Easy enough, right? I folded the map and slid it into the incredibly cool duffel with a patchwork of jewel-tone fabrics, beads, and tiny circular mirrors stitched on it that I'd purchased from a street vendor in Covent Garden. And honestly? When we landed, Jim, Jen, and I unfolded that little piece of paper, took the train, found the Naf Naf store and the two-star hotel across from it with the bathroom down the hall, and checked in. We never for a second questioned if we would find Hotel L'Europa or if there would be a vacancy that night for us. We felt like seasoned travelers living the dream. We had zero idea what we were doing. But we fully trusted Mark. We never doubted his authority—he'd been to Paris before. Or his intentions—he was our friend and would of course direct us to someplace safe. If Mark said we should get off at the Saint-Michel metro stop, we should. If he told us Hotel L'Europa was a safe place to stay, we believed him.

We were so quick to trust Mark sending us off to Paris, where there are more than three hundred metro stops and over sixteen hundred hotels, and we just assumed the ones he told us about were the correct ones—that his instructions would work. So why oh why are we so hesitant to trust that Jesus will show us where to go, what job to interview for, what schools to apply to, if we should date that person, or if we should rent or buy?

King David writes in Psalm 25,

> Show me your ways, LORD,
>   teach me your paths.
> Guide me in your truth and teach me,
>   for you are God my Savior,
>   and my hope is in you all day long.
>   (vv. 4–5)

Do we, like King David, ask God to teach us His paths? To guide us? Or do we wing it? Stress out about it? Agonize over the decisions?

Maybe we ask for or follow advice from our sister-in-law, that lady in the pickup line whose hair always looks so cute, or the influencer we follow on social media. But why do we go to them before Jesus? Not that those people will necessarily steer us wrong. And their advice does have a time and a place. Our sister-in-law might have great insight into which family traditions are important at Thanksgiving and what Gramma's secret recipe for sweet potato casserole is. The gal with the darling hair could probably recommend a great stylist, and the musician we follow most likely has some solid suggestions for other bands we might enjoy. But trusting those folks about life decisions would be like asking my mom, who had never been to France, which metro to take and where I should stay in Paris. I ask my mom for advice on plenty of things, but . . .

Where do you go for advice?

When it comes to the best way to deal with your friend's alcoholism. Should you confront her? If so, when? How can you show her love and support while suggesting she get help? Or what about whether you should quit your day job to pursue your passion? Or is that activity, show, or habit okay for you to partake in? Or how are you possibly going to move on after you lost someone you love?

Those are really complex questions, super important to get the very best advice about. And the best advice comes from the Lord.

> Good and upright is the LORD;
>   therefore he instructs sinners in his ways.
> He guides the humble in what is right
>   and teaches them his way.
> All the ways of the LORD are loving and
>   faithful. (vv. 8–10)

The Lord is the one who can give us the best advice, the one who instructs, guides, and teaches us in a loving and faithful way. He wants what's best for us, what's healthiest for us, what's most life-giving for us.

How do we know we can trust Him? Because He created us. He loves us. He died for us.

> Guard my life and rescue me;
>   do not let me be put to shame,
>   for I take refuge in you.
> May integrity and uprightness protect me,
>   because my hope, LORD, is in you.
>   (vv. 20–21)

I know all this, but I'm still guilty of sometimes doubting Jesus. Of trying to do it all on my own. Two examples come to mind of when I seriously questioned God's plans for my life. They are now important reminders of why I should always trust God's directions.

1. "Why did we break up, God? I *really* liked him."
2. "Hmm, no, God, actually I wanted to go to college in Virginia. Why didn't I get into this school?"

Breakups are painful. But God reminded me through the Bible that He loves me (John 3:16). That He will never leave or forsake me (Hebrews 13:5). And it turns out those guys from the breakups (yes, plural) were not the guys for me. God had always intended for me to marry Brett. I couldn't see that yet, but God could. And if those relationships, the ones that ended badly, had continued, I would have missed out on the beautiful life Brett and I share. So even in the midst of those heartbreaking moments, God was actually guarding my life and showing me His ways (Psalm 25:4, 20).

And although I wanted to go to college in Virginia, God wanted me to go to school in Ohio, so I could meet Brett. If I had gotten accepted at my first pick, University of Virginia, well, my life might have looked very different. But God not only told me to go to a different "metro stop," Miami of Ohio, but He also temporarily closed the UVA metro stop so I couldn't go that way if I tried.

Time after time Jesus points me back to who He is, to why I should trust Him, to what's best in a specific situation, even if I don't like it in the moment. Jesus only leads us to light. Never to destruction or dark places. This is one of the ways we can confirm if what we heard is from God. Was that nudge you felt toward light or dark? Jesus tells us in John 8:12, "I am the light of the world. Whoever follows me will never walk in darkness, but will have the light of life." We can trust Jesus as our guide.*

And because Jesus is the truth, He never lies and is always right. One hundred percent. Brett and I have been married for twenty-six years, living a beautiful romance. And we now live in the town in Ohio where we both went to school. Did I mention Brett's a professor here? Talk about God's perfect map of how things should look.

Living in a college town, I end up in all kinds of conversations with university students who are terrified about their futures. They put enormous amounts of pressure on themselves to get everything perfect upon graduation. They want to move to the city of their dreams, work in a field they're passionate about, make a ton of money, and live with their favorite friend in an adorable apartment that looks like the set of the television show *Friends*. It would also be great if they could get engaged soon to the perfect guy—is it the guy they're dating? How will they know? They'd like to be engaged for one and a half years, living on their own, and then get married. In June. Outside. On a sunny day. With pale-blue bridesmaids dresses.

Which are all great dreams. But these awesome students are so worried about getting it all right on their own that they forget they have the perfect guide for their lives. I often ask them, "Have you prayed about it?"

---

* For more on hearing from God, see the appendix in the back of the book.

And these students, who I know are Christians, look at me blankly. Then stutter, "I mean, kind of, well, not exactly. I mean, I just really hope I get the interview, and did I mention I don't want to live too far away from home?"

I'm not trying to pick on these students. I already shared some of the ways I've doubted the Almighty, despite His almightiness. We're all guilty of trying to take things into our own hands. I'm guessing you've questioned God or put your wish list ahead of His a few times too. But when we remember that God sees the future and knows the ideal way things should go, that He wants the very best for us, and that He has the power to make the perfect plan come to fruition, then we can reset our minds to trust Him.

> Who, then, are those who fear the LORD?
>   He will instruct them in the ways they
>   should choose.
> They will spend their days in prosperity,
>   and their descendants will inherit the land.
> The LORD confides in those who fear him;
>   he makes his covenant known to them.
>   (Psalm 25:12–14)

Fearing the Lord does not mean being afraid of Him. It means being in awe of Him. Accepting Jesus as our king, as our authority. The psalmist says if we are in awe of God and trust Him as our authority, just like I trusted my friend Mark to be an authority on where we should stay in Paris, then God will instruct us in the ways we should choose—in our jobs, homes, relationships, and conversations. He makes the right paths known to us—never hides them, never tries to speak to us in code, and never keeps the correct choices hidden. Why? Because like my friend Mark, God wants us to find our way, to enjoy the city He sends us to, to be kept safe, to be surrounded by people who point us back to Jesus and His love.

On that first trip to France, my classmates and I had no idea how to get to Paris two days prior to going there, but the day before, when the time was right, Mark gave us everything we needed to get the most out of our jaunt across the English Channel. Because Mark told us right before our trip, his directions were fresh in our minds. He gave us a map to follow. And he spoke to three of us.

Jesus does this for us and more. When the time is right, He'll reveal the information we need to make the next steps in our journeys. He gives us the map of the Bible to direct us throughout our travels, so we can refer back to it to confirm if where we think we should go matches with God's holy, loving character and His perfect plans. Jesus also shows others His itinerary for us if necessary. If we're supposed to get married, God will let the person we're supposed to marry know that we're the one for them. God will close the doors to jobs and schools and situations that wouldn't be best for us (like those ex-boyfriends of mine and my UVA application). He'll let the employer who is supposed to hire us know that we're the perfect person for the job during our interview. If grad school is God's perfect plan for us, He will nudge the admissions officer of the school where God leads us to accept the application we pored and prayed over. But we have to be listening. That whole "fear of the Lord" thing means we need to (as we talked about in the first chapter) be abiding in Jesus, thrilling on His words. When we do that we can read God's map with more clarity, be more in tune with the people God places on our paths, and be more wary of anything or anyone that might lead us astray.

Mark was a great guy. I remember he was usually smiling. He was super creative and a captivating storyteller. But I haven't seen him since college. If I totally trusted him to get me to a foreign country, shouldn't I trust that Jesus will get me where I need to go? Thinking about who you've trusted for advice in the past, your "Marks," shouldn't you trust the King of the universe to direct your path? To be your authority? We never have to question, wonder, or doubt if Jesus will show us the way, because Jesus is the Way. In Him we can fully put our trust.

──────── RESTORE ────────

Do you have any big decisions for which you're trying to discern God's will?

Write out a life path you're trying to discern. Set a timer for sixty seconds. Spend the entire minute praying for God's direction on this thing. Commit to doing the same thing every day this week. Throughout the week, make sure you jot down anything you read, see, or hear that feels like God giving you direction. At the end of the week, write in big letters on the page with your question, "Jesus will instruct me in the ways I should choose."

10

TREE HOUSE

Psalm 27

The LORD is my light and my salvation—
whom shall I fear?
The LORD is the stronghold of my life—
of whom shall I be afraid?

When the wicked advance against me
to devour me,
it is my enemies and my foes
who will stumble and fall.
Though an army besiege me,
my heart will not fear;
though war break out against me,
even then I will be confident.

One thing I ask from the LORD,
this only do I seek:
that I may dwell in the house of the LORD
all the days of my life,
to gaze on the beauty of the LORD
and to seek him in his temple.
For in the day of trouble
he will keep me safe in his dwelling;
he will hide me in the shelter of his sacred tent
and set me high upon a rock.

Then my head will be exalted
above the enemies who surround me;

at his sacred tent I will sacrifice with shouts
of joy;
I will sing and make music to the LORD.

Hear my voice when I call, LORD;
be merciful to me and answer me.
My heart says of you, "Seek his face!"
Your face, LORD, I will seek.
Do not hide your face from me,
do not turn your servant away in anger;
you have been my helper.
Do not reject me or forsake me,
God my Savior.
Though my father and mother forsake me,
the LORD will receive me.
Teach me your way, LORD;
lead me in a straight path
because of my oppressors.
Do not turn me over to the desire of my foes,
for false witnesses rise up against me,
spouting malicious accusations.

I remain confident of this:
I will see the goodness of the LORD
in the land of the living.
Wait for the LORD;
be strong and take heart
and wait for the LORD.

There were two predominant trees in my childhood. Both of them were willow trees. One I mentioned in the chapter on Psalm 23 in the field where I played. The other was in our side yard. Its branches looked like they were dripping, like a waterfall of silvery green. Inside those branches I was almost invisible to the outside world. I felt safe there. Like no one could find or touch me.

That tree was my secret hiding place. The place I could

go when I needed to get away from everything but had no way of going anywhere a bike couldn't carry me because I was thirteen.

When the world said I was too old to play make-believe but my mind wanted to imagine fairies with glittery wings and dragons with shimmery scales.

When it seemed no one understood me.

When my heart hurt and I felt tears stinging the corners of my eyes but didn't want anyone to see.

When the raised voices of my parents echoed in my bones.

I could escape to my willow tree. A place where I felt God's peace. Where I saw the beauty of His creation. Where I could take deep breaths and recalibrate.

King David wrote Psalm 27, and in it he asks God for this kind of safe place:

> One thing I ask from the LORD,
>   this only do I seek:
> that I may dwell in the house of the LORD
>   all the days of my life,
> to gaze on the beauty of the LORD
>   and to seek him in his temple. (v. 4)

King David also sought safe shelter. Sure, this psalm was most likely written while David was being chased through the wilderness by an angry king, and I was just a scrawny middle school girl with thick rainbow-colored glasses and braces. But, come on—middle school is the worst, wrought with identity struggles and insecurities. I needed shelter. We all do.

> For in the day of trouble
>   he will keep me safe in his dwelling;
> he will hide me in the shelter of his sacred
>   tent
>   and set me high upon a rock. (v. 5)

We all have things we fear. The dentist's chair. A meeting with our boss. Spiders. Someone who threatens our well-being. Or the well-being of someone we love. Not being able to pay our bills. Addiction. The dark. And we all have days of trouble. The day in court. The confrontation. The diagnosis. The argument. The loss. And when these fears materialize, when our days of trouble come, we have a protector, a place to go—we can go to Jesus.

> The LORD is my light and my salvation—
>   whom shall I fear?
> The LORD is the stronghold of my life—
>   of whom shall I be afraid? (v. 1)

King David wrote this psalm like a simple logical proof. Even I, who way prefer words to numbers, can follow this one.

A. God is my light.

B. God is my salvation.

C. Therefore, with God brightening my ways and saving me, I have nothing to fear.

If A is true and B is true, then C is true: I have nothing to be afraid of.

Let's work that out through Scripture.

God is light

> In [Jesus] was life, and that life was the light of all mankind. The light shines in the darkness, and the darkness has not overcome it. (John 1:4–5)

> When Jesus spoke again to the people, he said, "I am the light of the world." (John 8:12)

God is my salvation

> If you declare with your mouth, "Jesus is Lord," and believe in your heart that God raised him from the dead, you will be saved. (Romans 10:9)

> For God so loved the world that he gave his one and only Son, that whoever believes in him shall not perish but have eternal life. (John 3:16)

One more time, if A, God is our light, is true, and B, God is our salvation, is true, then C, we can (as the Bible instructs over and over again) fear not! Because when things feel scary, our Light and Salvation named Jesus steps in to provide us protection.

Jesus promises us a life where we don't need to be afraid of what happened in the past, of what we found out just now, or of what might happen someday along the road. Will this life be perfect? Nope. There will still be scary things for sure. And when they come, Jesus will save us. Yes, He saves our very souls. And that is incredible. Jesus is the light that leads us and protects us from darkness.

In Deuteronomy 31:6 God instructs and promises us, "Be strong and courageous. Do not be afraid or terrified because of [your enemies], for the LORD your God goes with you; he will never leave you nor forsake you."

And in Isaiah 41:10 God says, "So do not fear, for I am with you; do not be dismayed, for I am your God. I will strengthen you and help you; I will uphold you with my righteous right hand."

God promises to never leave us (Hebrews 13:5–6). Not in our depression or abuse or anything else. That could mean if we're suffering from depression, Jesus will point us to a therapist who can help us walk through it. Or when home life is horrible, God might open a classroom after school where the teacher listens so well, always has snacks, and lets us stay as long as we like until we feel ready to brave going home. I have a friend going through something unthinkable who escapes to a nearby stream. She can walk there from her house. And as she prays through what she should do, she has a protected place to sit and sigh and cry. She tells me she feels God's love and peace there. She believes God put it there just for her.

I believe God provides ways out and people who help us out, but I also believe there are actual places He gives us for shelter. For me it happened to be a gorgeous willow tree I could climb into whenever middle school Laura felt shaky. A place where the sunlight danced through the silvery leaves, where squirrels chattered as they cracked acorns open in their tiny paws, where the breeze seemed to exhale the fear, pain, and uncertainty and allowed me to regain my strength, to take heart, to wait for the Lord.

For you this could be your closet or front porch. Stepping out of one place and into a change of scenery, with different lighting and sound, can be a great reprieve. My mom likes to sit in her sunroom. In the Harry Potter books, Harry, Ron, and Hermione scurried off to Hagrid's hut for advice or a safe place to chat. Pooh Bear had his Thoughtful Spot where he could sit on a log and parse out ideas. Maybe God will show you a trail where you can get away from the noise of your life and bike and breathe in fresh air. There might be an old church near you that keeps its doors open and allows passersby to sit in silence in wooden pews, speckled with colorful designs of light as it filters through stained glass. Perhaps there's a park bench where you can rest and reflect, or maybe even a tree to climb. I'm certain God has a place for you. You might need to do some searching. Some trial and error. Talk to Him about it. He wants you to find it.

When I was ready—whether that meant I'd played pretend, sang some of my favorite songs, had a good cry, or just sat and let the magical light shifting between the long, thin, swaying boughs soothe me like a massage for my soul—I'd climb down from my willow tree's branches and slip back inside. I always felt like Jack and Annie stepping out of their magic tree house that acted as a time machine for their adventures. It seemed no one ever noticed I'd been gone, as if no time had passed whatsoever. No one ever asked where I'd been.

I believe God gave me that space—that He hid me in the shelter of His sacred tent (v. 5). It provided solace for me in a time when my dad moved out and back home and back out again. When the floors in our house felt unsteady. When the things I'd always believed seemed wispy.

I believe God heard my cry, that He did not hide His face from me. That He did not reject or forsake me but received me (vv. 7–9). He set my feet on a solid and beautiful tree trunk. He strengthened and nourished my soul even though I didn't know what it was I needed. And I believe He will do it again, should I ever need a shelter. I believe He will do it for you too. Because God is so many things, and one of them is a protector.

RESTORE

Do you have a safe place you go when the world feels upside down?

If so, go there today. Even if your life feels upright. Thank God for providing you a shelter. Breathe in His peace.

If not, ask God to reveal to you how He wants to keep you safe. Ask Him for a place where you can vent and still your soul.

11

IF YOU JUMP, I JUMP

Psalm 31

In you, LORD, I have taken refuge;
let me never be put to shame;
deliver me in your righteousness.
Turn your ear to me,
come quickly to my rescue;
be my rock of refuge,
a strong fortress to save me.
Since you are my rock and my fortress,
for the sake of your name lead and guide me.
Keep me free from the trap that is set for me,
for you are my refuge.
Into your hands I commit my spirit;
deliver me, LORD, my faithful God.

I hate those who cling to worthless idols;
as for me, I trust in the LORD.
I will be glad and rejoice in your love,
for you saw my affliction
and knew the anguish of my soul.
You have not given me into the hands of the
enemy
but have set my feet in a spacious place. . . .

How abundant are the good things
that you have stored up for those who fear
you,
that you bestow in the sight of all,
on those who take refuge in you.

In the shelter of your presence you hide them
from all human intrigues;
you keep them safe in your dwelling
from accusing tongues.

Praise be to the LORD,
for he showed me the wonders of his love
when I was in a city under siege.
In my alarm I said,
"I am cut off from your sight!"
Yet you heard my cry for mercy
when I called to you for help.

Love the LORD, *all his faithful people!*
The LORD *preserves those who are true to*
him,
but the proud he pays back in full.
Be strong and take heart,
all you who hope in the LORD. *(vv. 1–8,*
19–24)

There's an iconic scene in one of my all-time favorite movies, *Titanic*, where Rose, a well-to-do socialite, is determined to end her life. She and her mother have lost their wealth, and in order to maintain their existing quality of living (translation: gorgeous gowns, exquisite jewelry, and traveling first class on the luxurious "Queen of the Ocean," which would cost approximately fifty thousand dollars per ticket today), Rose's mother insists she marry rich, and not just any rich guy but a particular rich guy who happens to be a jerk.

A quick glance at her future looks like living miserably ever after, so in desperation Rose climbs the rail of the *Titanic*, planning to jump. A steerage passenger named Jack spies Rose and calls from behind, "Don't do it!"[7]

Jack explains that if she jumps, he'll jump. To him, it's not an option. Jack tells Rose, "I'm involved now. You let go, I'm going to have to jump in after you."

Rose wasn't calling out for help, well, not out loud. But anyone contemplating suicide is crying out in their heart for rescue from something. Jack Dawson, portrayed by Leonardo DiCaprio, does a pretty stellar job on-screen of talking Rose out of jumping and guiding her to turn toward him and give him her hand.

Jesus does this for us, but even better. He is the one who hears our heart's cry of fear, loneliness, desperation. The one who sees us on the edge of destruction, at the end of our rope, and says, "Don't do it."

If we dismiss Him or tune Him out, Jesus says, "If you let go, I'm going to jump in after you." Jesus never wonders, Hmm, should I help my beloved child who I created or not? Will I get wet? Will the water be bitter cold? Is it worth it?

No. Our God doesn't think like that.

He sees any of His children—that's you and me—in trouble, and Jesus reminds us that we're loved and cherished. If we don't believe His kind words or are in too dark of a place to hear them, Jesus starts tugging off His boots so He's ready to jump into deep waters if we choose them. And if we're still reluctant, Jesus reaches out His almighty hand and offers us refuge.

King David, who wrote Psalm 31, most likely while he was being pursued by King Saul, knew this:

> Turn your ear to me,
>   come quickly to my rescue;
> be my rock of refuge,
>   a strong fortress to save me.
> Since you are my rock and my fortress,
>   for the sake of your name lead and guide
>   me.

Keep me free from the trap that is set for me,
for you are my refuge. (vv. 2–4)

Have you ever been here? Felt trapped? Or maybe you're here now in this season. In a place of danger. Fear. Out of ideas or money or strength or hope. Perhaps someone else made a horrible decision or series of horrible decisions that landed you here. Or maybe you're in a desperate place due to a broken system or a natural disaster. Your situation might make you feel like nobody can see you, but Jesus does. We can call out to Him, and He will hear us. What King David declared, we can too:

In my alarm I said,
"I am cut off from your sight!"
Yet you heard my cry for mercy
when I called to you for help. (v. 22)

Will you cry out to Jesus?

Sometimes we bring hardship on ourselves. We get to a place where we want to quit doing the thing we know we shouldn't do, but we slip. When we really want to stop our disordered eating, addiction, spending, or anger, but something trips us up. Like the apostle Paul declared to the early church in Italy, "I don't really understand myself, for I want to do what is right, but I don't do it. Instead, I do what I hate" (Romans 7:15 NLT). Even then, Jesus is still gripping our wrists. We can commit ourselves to His hands, because they are strong and they are faithful.

"Into your hands I commit my spirit; deliver me, LORD, my faithful God," David proclaimed (v. 5).

These are also the exact words of Jesus on the cross found in Luke 23:46: "Father, into your hands I commit my spirit."

Sit with that a moment.

King David trusted God. Jesus trusted His heavenly Father (and His equal along with the Holy Spirit as part of the Trinity) even in total agony on the cross. If David could trust God while the current king had a bounty on his head, if Jesus could trust God with nails in His wrists and feet, if David's plea, Christ's main thought—the one He spoke out loud—was "I give up, but, God, I trust you," shouldn't we consider also committing ourselves, entrusting ourselves, to God's hands?

What would it take for you to trust God today?

What's stopping you?

Hanging off the edge of a ship with our feet dangling over the icy sea is terrifying. Back up on the ship's deck we might still have to face whatever it is that brought us here, but we can breathe again, because we have the option to face that thing with Jesus by our side. Will life be perfect as soon as we cry out to the Lord, as soon as we agree to trust Him?

Probably not. But it will be better.

One friend who wishes she were married decided to trust God with her singleness. She's still single and some days she feels painful aches of loneliness, but God has opened her eyes to the great friendships she has, to the beauty around her, to His faithfulness. She often tells me she has such a blessed life.

I've seen other friends get checks in the mail for the exact dollar amount they needed to make ends meet that month. I have a friend who was living in a destructive relationship without anywhere safe to go. Then, just at the pivotal moment, someone took in her and her kiddos, providing safety and security. I've listened to a single mom applaud the men in her small group who have taught her son how to change a flat tire and fix a leaky faucet—things she doesn't know how to do and that she worried her son would never learn. Like the psalmist, even though these friends found themselves in desolate places, they can declare that God has set their feet in spacious places (Psalm 31:8). God has an abundance of good things stored up for you too (v. 19). Even in the hard times. He loves you.

I love *The Message* version of the final line of this psalm: "Be brave. Be strong. Don't give up. Expect GOD to get here soon" (v. 24).

Hold on to that today. Be brave. Be strong. Don't give up. God hears you and He's running across the deck of the ship to rescue you. You can trust Him with every aspect of your life, your very life. Take His hand. Don't worry about slipping. He's got you. He'll never let go.

———————— RESTORE ————————

Is there anything in your life that makes you feel trapped, alone, or ready to give up?

Ask Jesus for courage. Right now. Out loud. Ask Him to make you strong. Ask Him for endurance.

Picture yourself reaching out to Jesus, His strong, capable, loving hands holding on to you and pulling you to safety.

12

SHARING THE HARD STUFF

Psalm 32

Blessed is the one
  whose transgressions are forgiven,
  whose sins are covered.
Blessed is the one
  *whose sin the L*ORD *does not count against*
     them
  and in whose spirit is no deceit.

When I kept silent,
  my bones wasted away
  through my groaning all day long.
For day and night
  your hand was heavy on me;
my strength was sapped
  as in the heat of summer.

Then I acknowledged my sin to you
  and did not cover up my iniquity.
I said, "I will confess
  *my transgressions to the L*ORD."
And you forgave
  the guilt of my sin.

Therefore let all the faithful pray to you
  while you may be found;
surely the rising of the mighty waters
  will not reach them.

You are my hiding place;
you will protect me from trouble
and surround me with songs of deliverance.

I will instruct you and teach you in the way
you should go;
I will counsel you with my loving eye on
you.
Do not be like the horse or the mule,
which have no understanding
but must be controlled by bit and bridle
or they will not come to you.
Many are the woes of the wicked,
but the LORD's unfailing love
surrounds the one who trusts in him.

Rejoice in the LORD and be glad, you
righteous;
sing, all you who are upright in heart!

As I prepared to speak at my first women's confer-ence, I walked through my talk with a trusted friend. She challenged me, "Why should they listen to you? Why will they believe you?"

I inhaled sharply, opened my mouth to say something, but my throat felt thick. Heat flushed my face in shame. Did she not think I could do this?

I had wondered myself, but I believed I was supposed to share about finding our identity in Christ. For years I'd struggled with my own self-worth, and God had taught me so much about how He specifically designs each of us—how He literally gets excited when we rock what we've got instead of trying to be more like someone else and less like ourselves (Galatians 6:4–5). I wanted to share this revelation with whoever would listen and felt God was calling me to do so. But now my friend, who'd sat through Bible studies I'd taught at our church, was questioning my credentials.

She continued, "I mean, sure, you're a gifted teacher, and your message is important, but the women are going to look at you and think, That skinny blonde girl is happily married with four kids and still managed to put on a cute outfit and makeup. There's no way she can understand my struggles. She has it all together. I do not. She can't relate to my situation at all."

"But I *don't* have it all together," I whined.

My friend laughed. "How will they know that? Unless you tell them."

Zing.

I wanted to share the wonderful ways our Creator made and loves us, but I hesitated to share the ugly things from my past, the scars from being belittled and manipulated, the desperate, sinful things I did to try to get attention and earn love, the wounds formed because of those sins. I worried what people would think about me if they saw the dark parts of my soul.

Don't we all? But unless we share, we can't heal. And unless we share, how are we going to invite others into Christ's grace?

King David knew how harmful it can be to hold our hurts inside. He wrote about it in Psalm 32.

> When I kept silent,
>   my bones wasted away
>   through my groaning all day long.
> For day and night
>   your hand was heavy on me;
> my strength was sapped
>   as in the heat of summer. (vv. 3–4)

But David also knew the relief and freedom of admitting his sins.

> Then I acknowledged my sin to you
>   and did not cover up my iniquity.
> I said, "I will confess
>   my transgressions to the LORD."
> And you forgave
>   the guilt of my sin. (v. 5)

My friend was one hundred percent right. I had to apply this to my Bible teaching—an honesty, a transparency, that said, "Hey, I'm not perfect. I'm not here to tell you how it's done. I'm here to tell you how God works, about His grace. I took the wrong paths, and felt the pain of the consequences. Growing up I was told I was ugly, awkward, clumsy, dumb, and not enough. I believed these lies, felt rejected and worthless. I tried to earn love and approval. I did things I'm not proud of to try to fill the void inside. I am a sinner. But a grateful one. Because Christ's forgiveness and love changed me. It is because of His amazing grace that I stand here in front of you, actually loving who He created me to be."

When I got vulnerable onstage, woman after woman came up afterward to tell me their stories. They too had been told they didn't measure up. They too had believed the lies. They too had done things they'd regretted. Some of them were still in the thick of doing those things. Some of them, like me, had found new life in the unconditional love Jesus offers. But all of us who dared to speak truth created a place where darkness got shut down, because we let the light shine on it. And the light was contagious.

Me confessing my not-so-pretty past helped others share theirs, and together we squelched the lies Satan was trying to tell us about who we are, moving forward to own who Christ says we are—loved, redeemed, priceless, forgiven. His sons and daughters.

These conversations aren't easy, but the psalmist reminds us, "You [God] are my hiding place; you protect me from trouble. You surround me with songs of victory" (v. 7 NLT).

Which means that even though we may be tempted to appear to be the "perfect Christian," (1) there's no such thing, and (2) God is singing and celebrating the win, the freedom we're stepping into. There is triumph in telling the truth and unlocking the shameful trap that the chains of unconfessed sin hold us in.

The same holds true in friendships. The best ones are not the ones with people who put on a facade of having it all together. My closest friendships are with women who are honest with me and with whom I feel safe being transparent. We share our best and worst days with each other, sometimes in the same breath. Because it is in the transparency that together we can find freedom from sin and celebrate God's goodness in our lives.

When friends share with me their parenting, marriage, or self-image challenges, it breaks down the false perception that their lives are perfect, despite the cute vacation pics they posted last week. It frees me up to confess how I handled a situation with one of my kids extremely poorly and how I got jealous about someone else's success. I can share in a safe space where I'm protected by my God and the trusted people He's put in my life. I can process where I'm failing, get perspective as my confidants remind me that Jesus forgives this and all sin, and get prayers for help and support in the struggle.

We as a culture shy away from conversations that make us look weak, vulnerable, or wrong. We want to project an image that's bright and shiny. But when we do, all the ick festers inside like pus in a wound. Sorry, I grossed myself out too, but it really is that bad. No one wants to announce, "I messed up!"

What is it you don't want anyone to know?

Satan wants us to think we should keep all the hard, ugly stuff inside. Whether that's our sins or someone else's sins or harmful accusations against us or just the ugly circumstances we find ourselves in. The enemy wants to shame us into thinking we won't be forgiven, we won't be loved, people will think the worst of us, our lives will be over. Lie. Lie. Lie. Lie.

Jesus died for us on the cross. When He did that He took all our sins. Every. Single. One. The sins from our past, the sin we find ourselves in today, the ways we'll mess up eight years from now. Sharing our failures won't stop His forgiveness, can't stop it. It's already done. Two-thousand-years-ago done.

We are loved. Jesus loves us. John 3:16 tells us that God sent Jesus to earth because He loves us. Jesus instructed us in John 13:34 to "love one another . . . as *I have loved* you" (emphasis added). First John 4:18 reminds us that Jesus's perfect love casts out fear.

So:

1. Christ's love is perfect and can't be marred or smeared or dissolved by our addictions, abandonments, anger issues, allergies, or aunt's opinion.

2. This love shoves out any reason to fear getting things out in the open. Because Jesus's love says, "I already know every skeleton you're hiding in your closet and love you endlessly. You may as well get them out there, deal with them, not let them take space in your life or haunt you anymore, because hiding those skeletons is doing us absolutely no good."

If you're afraid of something, if you're ashamed of something, if you're shouldering a diagnosis, a financial burden, being let go from your job, an ugly episode from season one of your life, what's stopping you from sharing it? And let's be clear, this does not mean sharing with everyone you meet, big groups, the internet, or at the grocery store. It means sharing with a couple of trusted individuals and with God. God already knows all about it, but He'd love to hear it from you so the two of you can work through it together. Because God loves you, He might just use a friend, counselor, pastor, or sibling to help you in your hour of need.

Paul tells us in Romans 8:1, "There is now no condemnation for those who are in Christ Jesus."

No condemnation.

None.

No matter what the enemy is trying to make you believe.

That doesn't mean there won't be any consequences. If you stole something, you should give it back. If you hurt someone, you should say you're sorry. If you shirked your responsibilities, it's time to step up and get back to work. If you're addicted to something, seek help. But despite any sin in your life, or its consequences, God still wants good things for you. His unfailing love surrounds you (v. 10). He's still on your side. He forgives you. All your guilt is gone (v. 5). You can sing for joy (v. 11).

—— RESTORE ——

Is there a sin, someone else's sin, or something else shameful or hard in your life that you're keeping inside?

Spend some time talking to God about it. Then ask Him to let you know of at least one safe person you might be able to share your burden with. End your prayer time reading Psalm 32 out loud, particularly verses 1 and 2, 5, and 11.

13

NEWS OF THE DAY

Psalm 37

*Do not fret because of those who are evil
   or be envious of those who do wrong;
for like the grass they will soon wither,
   like green plants they will soon die away.*

*Trust in the LORD and do good;
   dwell in the land and enjoy safe pasture.
Take delight in the LORD,
   and he will give you the desires of your
      heart.*

*Commit your way to the LORD;
   trust in him and he will do this:
He will make your righteous reward shine
      like the dawn,
   your vindication like the noonday sun.*

*Be still before the LORD
   and wait patiently for him;
do not fret when people succeed in their
      ways,
   when they carry out their wicked schemes.*

*Refrain from anger and turn from wrath;
   do not fret—it leads only to evil.
For those who are evil will be destroyed,*

but those who hope in the LORD will
*   inherit the land.*

A little while, and the wicked will be no more;
*   though you look for them, they will not be*
*   found.*
But the meek will inherit the land
*   and enjoy peace and prosperity. . . .*

For the power of the wicked will be broken,
*   but the LORD upholds the righteous.*

The blameless spend their days under the
*   LORD's care,*
*   and their inheritance will endure forever.*
In times of disaster they will not wither;
*   in days of famine they will enjoy plenty.*

But the wicked will perish:
*   Though the LORD's enemies are like the*
*   flowers of the field,*
*   they will be consumed, they will go up in*
*   smoke.*

The wicked borrow and do not repay,
*   but the righteous give generously;*
those the LORD blesses will inherit the land,
*   but those he curses will be destroyed.*

The LORD makes firm the steps
*   of the one who delights in him;*
though he may stumble, he will not fall,
*   for the LORD upholds him with his hand.*

I was young and now I am old,
*   yet I have never seen the righteous forsaken*
*   or their children begging bread. . . .*

Consider the blameless, observe the upright;
*   a future awaits those who seek peace.*
But all sinners will be destroyed;
*   there will be no future for the wicked.*

*The salvation of the righteous comes from
    the L*ORD;
  he is their stronghold in time of trouble.
*The L*ORD *helps them and delivers them;*
  *he delivers them from the wicked and saves
    them,*
*because they take refuge in him. (vv. 1–11,
    17–25, 37–40)*

I can't watch the news on television: the dramatic music—*dun dun dun*—leading headlines, and disturbing images of murder, abuse, corruption, and devastation stay with me for days. I'm extremely empathetic and visual, and the weight of all the trauma and turmoil in the world haunts me.

It's not just me. "More than half of Americans say the news causes them stress, and many report feeling anxiety, fatigue or sleep loss as a result," a survey from the American Psychological Association shows.[8] Even though we're not of this world, we do live in it.

So what do we do with all the ugliness? The name-calling politics? The hostility and suffering? Do we ignore the news?

No. But as Christians, we should process it through a bigger lens than our own—the lens that an almighty Creator and King cares and is in control.

Psalm 37 helps us do this. It turns our focus away from the turmoil in the world and back to the God of the universe who is good and just.

Do not fret because of those who are evil
  or be envious of those who do wrong;
for like the grass they will soon wither,
  like green plants they will soon die away.

Trust in the LORD and do good;
   dwell in the land and enjoy safe pasture.
Take delight in the LORD,
   and he will give you the desires of your
      heart. (vv. 1–4)

Did you see the 180 turn? David counsels us in this song he wrote not to worry about all the evildoers but instead to trust in the Lord. To stop dwelling and fretting about the news. To stop checking our feeds, flipping channels, refreshing our screens. To stop caring what he had to say about it or what she thought.

Our focus should be on God—on trusting Him.

Which is sometimes easier said than done. But David knew that.

King David wrote this psalm when he was an old man (v. 25). By this point in David's life, he had experienced his share of trials and tribulations. He'd been exiled and hunted down, lost both his best friend and his son to tragic deaths, and fought in multiple wars with a front-row seat to suffering and brutality. David doesn't tell us to live in a bubble and not pay attention to what's going on around us. He doesn't say we shouldn't be offended by malevolence or that we should ignore injustices. As a warrior, David relied on the news to defend his people from evil and unfairness. King David had spies all over the place so he would know what was going on both with his own people and in the lands around him (see 2 Samuel 15:13, 34, 37). But David tells us not to worry.

How? How can we not worry when all this pain prevails?

Because we can delight in the Lord.

David's instructions remind me of Jesus's consoling words to the disciples in John 16:33, "I have told you these things, so that in me you may have peace. In this world you will have trouble. But take heart! I have overcome the world."

Yup, Jesus says this world can be a painful place—full of trouble, but we're not supposed to wallow in those things. We should instead concentrate on Jesus—on His love, His light, His goodness—and when we do that, we can be of good cheer, we can delight in the fact that Jesus has overcome the world! In the midst of chaos, we can feel His peace that surpasses all understanding (Philippians 4:7).

Although some days it sounds dreamy to disregard the news, the Bible doesn't tell us to do that. It's important to know what's going on in the world. Jesus was fully aware of the corrupt political scene in Rome, Caesar's empire, the legalism of the Pharisees, the scope of Pilate's authority, and the underhanded ways of tax collectors. Our Savior knew what was going on around Him. And then He acted accordingly. Jesus instructed the disciples to pay their taxes to Rome (Mark 12:17). He called out the Pharisees when they were off base, and He invited tax collectors to change their ways. As followers of Jesus, we should take His lead—know what's going on and handle it to the best of our ability like Jesus would, obeying the rules when appropriate, calling people out when relevant, and inviting people who don't know Jesus out of their sin and into His love.

So when do we do which things? When do we take a stand and when do we sit quietly and pray for God's intervention? That depends.

A good place to start is by being informed. I subscribe to a daily news feed that highlights the top stories worldwide. Maybe you subscribe to a different one, or you prefer to check a certain website. My mom gets an actual newspaper delivered to her door each day. If a story feels particularly pertinent to me, I'll click on the link and check multiple sources I find reliable about that story. I can filter and process the news better this way—without it assaulting my senses and playing to all my overactive emotions.

Some news is just that—news. Someone won the Pulitzer Prize—amazing. The next Olympics will be held there—interesting. Cinnabon is now selling their frosting in tubs—where can I get some? I don't feel called to do anything with that news, except maybe order some of that frosting.

But other news is unthinkable—terrorist attacks, racial violence, child abuse, the sex trade. And in this kind of news, this horrific, heartbreaking news, we as Christians can pray—pray for healing and change and justice. *Jesus, why? Please help our world, Lord.* And our Lord, who is a healer, a game-changer, and a just judge, hears our prayers.

> Be still before the Lord
>   and wait patiently for him;
> do not fret when people succeed in their
>   ways,
>   when they carry out their wicked schemes.
>
> Refrain from anger and turn from wrath;
>   do not fret—it leads only to evil.
> For those who are evil will be destroyed.
>   (Psalm 37:7–9)

Instead of taking our ranting and complaining and finger-pointing to the bleachers, hallways, or dinner table, we can take them to the Lord. We can be still with Him. Sure, we can share our thoughts with trusted friends. But we can also talk to God and tell Him all our emotions. Really let them out. We can cry and scream and beg Him to change things. We can lean into the fact that the Lord despises evil. Verses 10 and 17 of this psalm reassure us:

A little while, and the wicked will be no
more;
though you look for them, they will not be
found . . .
for the power of the wicked will be broken.

We can allow the Prince of Peace to flood us with the reassurance that He is in control. He'll literally settle our hearts. We can ask Him for guidance on what to do. And in His faithfulness Jesus will direct us when He wants us to take action.*

When our community was heartbroken by the systemic racism in the news, a rally promoting kindness and inclusion was scheduled in our uptown park. My heart hurt for my African American friends. I wanted to show them support and learn more about what they were going through. Living in a college town, we frequently have rallies for all kinds of good causes. I don't feel tugged to attend all of them. If I did, I wouldn't be doing anything else with my time. But I felt Jesus pulling me to this particular event. I'd been praying for social justice. I'd been praying for healing for all those who had been hurt. And then this event, which aligned with God's instruction of loving our neighbors (Mark 12:31), popped up. I felt an immediate *you should go* kind of feeling. Within an hour my oldest daughter mentioned the event and asked if our family could all go. I brought it up to my husband. He'd also heard about the rally and agreed we should attend. When additionally our very busy calendar oddly had nothing scheduled that evening, it was clear to me I should be there. And so we went. Of course I didn't fix the systemic problem, but this was how God specifically directed me to deal with the news that was currently disturbing me.

---

* For more on hearing from God, see the appendix in the back of the book.

Another time God directed me on how to handle challenging news was during the last presidential election when there was great division between the two political parties. Ohio is a swing state, so we get barraged with all the ads, texts, and calls surrounding an election. Driving down the state highway to pick up my youngest from school every day, I was bombarded with dozens and dozens of political signs supporting multiple candidates, both parties, and different sides of the same issues. Passing those signs did something to me. They made me so angry—angry at the anger. So much judgment and hate on both sides from Christians and non-Christians alike. *Why, God? Why so much unkindness toward one another? Dear God, I pray for this election, that you will take care of our nation, our state, our city. I know you are in control . . . but, ick, this all feels so out of control.*

Then God redirected me: *Pray for unity.*

Okay.

I hadn't done that yet.

The Bible instructs us in Romans 12:18, "If it is possible, as far as it depends on you, live at peace with everyone." So this made total sense. It was biblical. I felt God specifically asking me, Laura Smith, to pray for unity in this situation. From that point on, every time I drove past those signs, instead of feeling all prickly and tense, instead of picking a side, I started praying for unity—for neighbors to love neighbors.

And I felt so much better. I was less flustered and more at peace. I also felt like I was actually doing something about an uneasy situation. When I stopped to "be still before the Lord," He helped me refocus on something productive, something for His kingdom.

God might have called you to react in completely different ways to both of these situations. Maybe even in reverse—to pray for those attending the rally and to attend an event for one of the candidates or issues to be voted on in the election. That's between you and God. But He will guide you. He desires goodness to rule and invites us, His people, into making the world a better place.

Sometimes God calls us to prayer and sometimes He calls us to action. When yet another hurricane hit Louisiana, countless locals volunteered to pass out blankets, food, and water. Others around the country were prompted to make financial donations to help the relief efforts. Churches throughout the United States prayed for those impacted by the storm. All of those were wonderful responses. God might nudge you to donate blood, organize a food drive, sign a petition, enlist in the armed services, write a check, repost an article, adopt a child, run for office, take up a collection, or take on any manner of things big or small to help right the wrongs in this evil world. And sometimes in the midst of terrifying news, God simply holds us in His gentle, loving arms.

Certainly not every time ugly news hits the wire do we get instructions from God on how to specifically handle that issue, but God knows us personally. And He knows each situation. He knows each step we take, every detail of our lives (Psalm 37:23). It's our job to call out to Him, to lean into Him, and when we do, when we're trusting God as the authority in our lives, then He'll direct our steps (v. 23).

In the midst of unsettling news, we should do the same thing we should do with everything else we experience—turn to the Lord. No matter what is making headlines, we can trust in our God. We can get riled up, excited, even fiery about fixing brokenness and making positive change. But Jesus tells us we don't have to be afraid. In the end, He wins. Jesus conquers all sin and wickedness. Until then, Jesus calls us into the battle against the evil of the world with Him—sometimes through prayer and sometimes through actions and sometimes through both. But He never wants us to be panicked about the news of the day.

Because our God is greater. Than a hurricane. A war. Human trafficking. Or anything else that might appear in your news feed tomorrow.

> The salvation of the righteous comes from
>   the LORD;
>   he is their stronghold in time of trouble.
> The LORD helps them and delivers them;
>   he delivers them from the wicked and
>   saves them,
>   because they take refuge in him.
>   (vv. 39–40)

RESTORE

How do you get the news? How often do you check the news?

Is there anything particular in the news right now that is causing you unease, stress, or worry? If so, write it down. If not, name something from previous news cycles that flustered or frightened you, or something else that triggers you.

Today you can create a healthy rhythm for processing news. Don't get overwhelmed. It barely takes any time and will help you be still and delight in the Lord.

1. Before you turn on your favorite news station or open your news feed, thank God for being almighty, sovereign, and just.

2. After reading the news, pray through any issues that tugged at your heart or were particularly concerning.

114

3. Ask God to still your heart and thoughts.

4. Ask Him if there's anything He wants you to do in response to your feelings and concerns. Some days that will be nothing. On others He'll just want you to breathe in His peace or maybe pray. Every now and then you will be called into action, but that's so cool because that's God inviting you to help Him fix our broken world.

5. Repeat tomorrow. And the day after that.

14

A ROCK TO STAND ON

Psalm 40

I waited patiently for the LORD;
he turned to me and heard my cry.
He lifted me out of the slimy pit,
out of the mud and mire;
he set my feet on a rock
and gave me a firm place to stand.
He put a new song in my mouth,
a hymn of praise to our God.
Many will see and fear the LORD
and put their trust in him.

Blessed is the one
who trusts in the LORD,
who does not look to the proud,
to those who turn aside to false gods.
Many, LORD my God,
are the wonders you have done,
the things you planned for us.
None can compare with you;
were I to speak and tell of your deeds,
they would be too many to declare.

Sacrifice and offering you did not desire—
but my ears you have opened—
burnt offerings and sin offerings you did
not require.
Then I said, "Here I am, I have come—

it is written about me in the scroll.
I desire to do your will, my God;
  your law is within my heart."

I proclaim your saving acts in the great
      assembly;
  I do not seal my lips, LORD,
  as you know.
I do not hide your righteousness in my heart;
  I speak of your faithfulness and your sav-
      ing help.
I do not conceal your love and your
      faithfulness
  from the great assembly.

Do not withhold your mercy from me, LORD;
  may your love and faithfulness always pro-
      tect me.
For troubles without number surround me;
  my sins have overtaken me, and I cannot
      see.
They are more than the hairs of my head,
  and my heart fails within me.
Be pleased to save me, LORD;
  come quickly, LORD, to help me.

May all who want to take my life
  be put to shame and confusion;
may all who desire my ruin
  be turned back in disgrace.
May those who say to me, "Aha! Aha!"
  be appalled at their own shame.
But may all who seek you
  rejoice and be glad in you;
may those who long for your saving help
      always say,
  "The LORD is great!"

But as for me, I am poor and needy;
  may the Lord think of me.

You are my help and my deliverer;
you are my God, do not delay.

Today I got invited to an event, and I was expected to attend. The problem? A person who emotionally manipulated and abused me would be there. I've spent years asking God to help me heal and forgive this person. I have Bible verses written out on a page in my journal that I go back to over and over again, reminding me of who God says I am to cancel out who this person tried to make me believe I was. I've let a few trusted friends and family into my struggle for support. I see a counselor to help me put language to what happened, process what I went through, and gain tools to move forward.

But the invite sent me reeling.

Some days I feel brave and unshakable, empowered by my almighty God, surrounded by His angel armies. But other days, even though God's courage and might are still available and His angels are all around, I slip and slide into a pit.

The invitation tangled my thinking. Thoughts rapid-fired through my brain and none of them were linear. I couldn't hold on to the bouncing thoughts or even put them into words. There was just a pervasive helplessness mixed with anger, fear, and worry. But mostly a feeling of *oh no, oh no, not again*, like I was falling into a hole without a rope.

I went for a run, worship music quiet in my ears as I tried to calm down, to process. But halfway around my neighborhood I felt like my feet wouldn't move. As if something was holding me to that spot.

And that's when God, as the psalmist writes, "inclined to me and heard my cry" (Psalm 40:1 ESV). He bent down and picked me up.

Again.

Because that's what our God does. No matter what pits we find ourselves in. Ones that we jumped into head-first because splashing in the mud looked like fun. Ones that we got shoved into against our will. And ones that we kind of slipped into because the ground was slimy.

It's as if King David knew my heart when he wrote this psalm.

> I waited patiently for the LORD;
>> he inclined to me and heard my cry.
> He drew me up from the pit of destruction,
>> out of the miry bog,
> and set my feet upon a rock,
>> making my steps secure.
> He put a new song in my mouth,
>> a song of praise to our God. (vv. 1–3 ESV)

I saw something shimmer out of the corner of my eye—just a flash. I took a breath and tried to start running again. But something tugged me back to that glint of light. I turned and noticed the large rock, maybe two by three feet, in a neighbor's yard. It had probably been there for years, but I'd never paid attention to it before. Lots of yards have decorative stones. But as my gaze fell on that large gray rock, the song in my earbuds was talking about standing on our Rock, Jesus, and I heard Him telling me I could stand on Him. He would keep me safe. He would make me strong.

Dismiss the whole incident if you like. But something made me slow down. Something caught my eye. And something caused me to gaze at a familiar rock in a whole new way at the exact moment those lyrics were playing. And for the first time since I'd gotten the distressing text, I felt hopeful. It felt a whole lot like Jesus protecting me and showing me how much He cares.

Jesus offers us a stable platform to stand on, bedrock to build our lives on no matter what comes our way. We just have to grab His hand when He reaches out, take Him up on that offer. Near the beginning of Jesus's ministry, He taught a crowd what the kingdom of God would look like, explaining:

> Therefore everyone who hears these words of mine and puts them into practice is like a wise man who built his house on the rock. The rain came down, the streams rose, and the winds blew and beat against that house; yet it did not fall, because it had its foundation on the rock. But everyone who hears these words of mine and does not put them into practice is like a foolish man who built his house on sand. The rain came down, the streams rose, and the winds blew and beat against that house, and it fell with a great crash. (Matthew 7:24–27)

As always, Jesus gives us a choice. We can build our lives on Him and His teachings. We can love our neighbors, seek Him first, not worry about tomorrow, do good, meaningful work, *and* rest from it. We can trust God with our relationships, our finances, and our futures. We can live lives where we listen to what Jesus says and put it into practice.

Or we can live however we want. We can go for the wrong guy or gal for the wrong reasons and strive for the awards and accolades of this world—the bigger check, house, or promotion, the most followers, likes, or fans. But when the storms of life come, we won't have anything to hold us up.

When there's a breakup or breakdown. When the company shuts down or the house burns down. What do we have left?

If we're living with Jesus and those same storms come, we still have hope. Because He is our hope. Jesus wants us to pick this choice—the one where we hear His words and put them into practice. The one where we sing the new song of praise He gives us.

Jesus knows this is easier said than done. He's not expecting us to be perfect. If we choose Jesus and we slip, because sometimes we will, He bends down and picks us up and gives us a do-over. He did it for the woman who was caught in the act of adultery. The angry crowd wanted to stone her. But Jesus told the trembling woman, who moments before had been staring shame and execution in the face, "Then neither do I condemn you. . . . Go now and leave your life of sin" (John 8:11).

Jesus also told a story about a disobedient son, who disowns his family and goes away and spends the family fortune on wild living (Luke 15:11–32). But when the son returns home in desperation, the father (who symbolizes God in the story) comes running out to hug his lost son and welcome him home. God is a God of second chances. The only catch? We need to want to build our lives on Him and His love.

I do want this. Because I've seen both sides—the pit and the rock. And I promise the rock is infinitely better. Sure, storms will come. They do. The phone rings and we can't control who is on the other end or what they may or may not say. But we can control how we'll handle it.

There will be repercussions if I don't go to the event I got invited to. Some people will be angry or disappointed or both with me. Others will talk about me behind my back. It's possible and probable that the man who manipulated me will try to find a way to use it as future fodder.

It's not easy going against the world's expectations or standing up to a bully. But I believe that Jesus will protect me, that He'll give me a firm place to stand. I feel Him saying, *Stay away from that pit, the event in question. The ground around it is slippery and could take you down. Instead, hold on to me. I'll keep you safe.*

And so, after much prayer and wise counsel, I've decided to hold on to Jesus and face the storm on my Rock. I'm not going to attend the event. I plan on avoiding the pit.

I, for one, want to handle this and everything else that comes my way with my feet planted firmly on granite, on something that won't give way, on something that is solid and constant and strong. Actually Someone, not something. Jesus promises to be all these things. For me and for you. He's done it before. And I fully trust that He will do it again.

RESTORE

Is there a pit you feel you're in or slipping toward?

Search for a real rock—a big one that you can stand on. Maybe in the woods or at a park or playground or outside a building. If you live somewhere where rocks are sparse, how about finding concrete steps or a stone park bench? Stand on it. Feel how solid it is. Imagine a windstorm or flood coming and how that rock would withstand it.

Right there on that rock, ask Jesus to be your rock. Reach out your hand in the air and invite Him to pull you up. Ask Him to help you stand strong in Him.

15

THIRSTY

Psalm 42

As the deer pants for streams of water,
so my soul pants for you, my God.
My soul thirsts for God, for the living God.
When can I go and meet with God?
My tears have been my food
day and night,
while people say to me all day long,
"Where is your God?"
These things I remember
as I pour out my soul:
how I used to go to the house of God
under the protection of the Mighty One
with shouts of joy and praise
among the festive throng.

Why, my soul, are you downcast?
Why so disturbed within me?
Put your hope in God,
for I will yet praise him,
my Savior and my God.

My soul is downcast within me;
therefore I will remember you
from the land of the Jordan,
the heights of Hermon—from Mount Mizar.
Deep calls to deep

in the roar of your waterfalls;
all your waves and breakers
have swept over me.

By day the LORD *directs his love,*
at night his song is with me—
a prayer to the God of my life.

I say to God my Rock,
"Why have you forgotten me?
Why must I go about mourning,
oppressed by the enemy?"
My bones suffer mortal agony
as my foes taunt me,
saying to me all day long,
"Where is your God?"

Why, my soul, are you downcast?
Why so disturbed within me?
Put your hope in God,
for I will yet praise him,
my Savior and my God.

What do you want? I mean really, really want. Like if you had a shiny golden genie lamp in your hand and got one wish, what would it be?

Think about it for a minute before you rub its burnished side.

No, you're not allowed to wish for more wishes. And you don't want to be like the foolish woodcutter in the fairy tale who was granted three wishes but due to a series of stubborn thoughts wasted his wishes on sausages. But that one thing that is always lingering somewhere in your mind. Think of that thing. Do you have it? Consider why you want it so badly.

Meaning, if what you want most is a new job, why is that?

Is it because money is tight and you'd like financial security? Maybe you should approach your boss about a raise or see if there's a way you could be scheduled for more hours or pick up an extra project. Or is it because the business you work for is shady and you feel uncomfortable working there knowing their practices? If so, maybe what you really want is to be upright, legal, and honest. Or maybe your boss is awful, not just unkind but downright mean and unfair. Then maybe what you're truly wishing for is to be respected, appreciated, treated well. Because a new boss would solve your problem—so a different job itself isn't truly your desire. Or is it because your best friend got a supercool job that makes yours seem boring? Because then you might just be jealous. Or perhaps God is prompting you to find a job that better utilizes the gifts He's given you.

If you're wishing for a relationship, engagement ring, or spouse, why do you think that is? Maybe you feel awkward third-wheeling it with your couple friends. Maybe you're uncomfortable traveling, driving home at night, or walking into a party solo. Maybe you want someone to share life with. Or don't want to be lonely. Perhaps you've watched too many Hallmark movies. Maybe it's all of the above.

Okay, let's take all those desires one step further: Why do we want to feel secure? Upright? Appreciated? Not lonely? Valued? Loved? Most humans want these things. I believe it's how God wired us. He put these desires deep in our hearts because there is something that provides us with all these things.

Him.

The Passion Translation of Psalm 42 begins like this:

> I long to drink of you, O God,
>   to drink deeply from the streams of
>   pleasure

flowing from your presence.
My longings overwhelm me for more of
    you!
My soul thirsts, pants, and longs for the liv-
    ing God. (vv. 1–2)

The psalmist knew what God offers—streams of plea-
sure, satisfaction for our longings. But are we going to
Jesus first to satisfy the innermost cravings of our soul?

The people I know who are currently looking for
jobs are stressing about their résumés, logging hours on
LinkedIn and Monster, and randomly applying for jobs
that aren't even something they'd enjoy doing. And yes,
I highly advise sprucing up your LinkedIn profile and
résumé prior to job hunting. Those are practical tactics.
But we also need to pray—talk to God about what He
has in store for us. Ask Him where He wants us to apply.
Beg Him to open doors He wants us to walk through
and close doors that conflict with His plan for us. Most
importantly we can thank God for being our ultimate
security and for giving us our true identity. Being created
in the image of God holds more clout than any title on
our email signature. Being loved by Him, adopted into
His family, gives us the true security we crave.

Some of my single friends think a significant other or
spouse will answer all their prayers, fill all their needs.
I'm here to tell them it's not true. I love being married.
My husband is my Prince Charming and best friend
rolled into one. Every day I feel incredibly blessed that I
get to do life with him. But even after twenty-six years of
marriage I still need to cling to Jesus as my identity, not
my husband. Yes, I am Brett's wife. And I wouldn't want
to be married to anyone else. But as great as Brett is, he's
human. And he can't understand all my thoughts or actions or be there for me 24/7. Jesus can.

Brett gives me love, support, encouragement, and

affection. But sometimes he's out of town and I'm left in our house to care for our kids and deal with the power outage and sleep in our bed solo. Some days he misunderstands me—thinks I wanted or meant one thing when I hoped for or tried to say something completely different. Some days Brett's plate is so full that he doesn't have the capacity to deal with my stuff too. When we're thirsty for love, Jesus is the water that never ever runs dry. No dating website, candlelit dinner, or diamond ring can quench your thirst. But Jesus's love will drench you.

I'm thirsty for my kids to be healthy, happy, and safe, for them to know the Lord, to do what's right. I'm also thirsty to have a wonderful, nurturing, loving relationship with them. If I get in an argument with one of my kids, my instinct is that I have a responsibility to resolve and reconcile it all on my own and quickly. Ha! What I need to do is go to Jesus. He calms my hyper emotions. He helps me see the whole picture better. What's going on with my child? What was the real issue we were arguing about? Should I have worded that differently? Do they need more space? Or more boundaries? Should I apologize or be more authoritative to direct their steps? Jesus answers these questions, guides my thoughts, and helps me be a better parent. But He also reminds me that I am His. That no matter how well or how badly I parent my kiddos I am loved by Him, and this is the most satisfying thing for my soul.

How about our hardest trials? Our times of desperation? What do we most want then?

When my husband experienced sharp internal pains and the doctor ordered an immediate MRI. The results of which could be devastating. I wanted to know if everything would be okay, no matter the diagnosis. I needed to be reminded that God would hold me either way, that He would hold our kids, that my husband would be at peace whether the results were good or horrific. The deepest part of my soul called out to God. And in my desperation and emptiness God flooded me with reassurance. As hot tears streamed down my cheeks, I knew we'd be all right—even if we got the worst news from the lab report. God promised to be with us. Somehow His love would prevail.

"Deep calls to deep," the psalmist declares (v. 7). When the deepest parts of our souls cry out for help, love, or redemption to the deepest heart of our Maker, God answers in a rush of love that covers us and fills our hearts.

"In the roar of your waterfalls; all your waves and breakers have swept over me" (v. 7). This is so beautiful. The psalmist reminds us that God's provision washes over us. That God's love sweeps over us like this. Waves and waterfalls and breakers gushing endless water. No matter how thirsty we are, this water isn't going to run dry.

The Bible tells us of a woman who was thirsty. She had her bucket in hand and was going to the well to get the water she needed for the day, as was customary for women in her time and place. Only she wasn't following the social norms. She came in the middle of the day when no one else would be there, when it was the hottest part of the day—the hardest time to come. Why?

Because this woman was thirsty for more than water. She was thirsty for belonging, for acceptance, for love, for a clean slate. Her past was painful. And Jesus was standing there waiting for her.

He told her, "Everyone who drinks this water [from the well] will be thirsty again, but whoever drinks the water I give them will never thirst. Indeed, the water I give them will become in them a spring of water welling up to eternal life" (John 4:13–14).

In a sermon about this Samaritan woman, Annie F. Downs said, "Our brokenness will take us back to the same wells over and over again until we realize they'll never satisfy."[9]

We can keep on going back to those wells. Or we can, as the psalmist instructs,

> Put [our] hope in God,
> for I will yet praise him,
> my Savior and my God. (Psalm 42:11)

We get to choose. Will we keep rubbing that genie lamp, hoping for answers to our wishes? Will we keep trying to do everything ourselves? Will we keep relying on the wells of the world—jobs, relationships, social media, bank accounts, home decor, status, even our health—to try to quench our thirst for security and love? Or will we go to Jesus and drink deeply of His living water that truly satisfies?

—— RESTORE ——

What are you truly thirsty for right now? Take that thing you'd wish for if you had a genie lamp and dig a bit deeper, and then a little deeper until you reveal your core motivation for wanting that thing.

Take that wish to Jesus. Let your deepest part call out to Him.

Now picture yourself approaching a waterfall and opening your mouth, or imagine yourself as a deer panting for water discovering a fresh, clear stream, and allow Jesus to quench your thirst with His love.

16

PIANO TUNING

Psalm 51

Have mercy on me, O God,
*   according to your unfailing love;*
according to your great compassion
*   blot out my transgressions.*
Wash away all my iniquity
*   and cleanse me from my sin.*

For I know my transgressions,
*   and my sin is always before me.*
Against you, you only, have I sinned
*   and done what is evil in your sight;*
so you are right in your verdict
*   and justified when you judge.*
Surely I was sinful at birth,
*   sinful from the time my mother con-*
*   ceived me.*
Yet you desired faithfulness even in the
*   womb;*
*   you taught me wisdom in that secret place.*

Cleanse me with hyssop, and I will be clean;
*   wash me, and I will be whiter than snow.*
Let me hear joy and gladness;
*   let the bones you have crushed rejoice.*
Hide your face from my sins
*   and blot out all my iniquity.*

Create in me a pure heart, O God,
and renew a steadfast spirit within me.
Do not cast me from your presence
or take your Holy Spirit from me.
Restore to me the joy of your salvation
and grant me a willing spirit, to sustain me.

Then I will teach transgressors your ways,
so that sinners will turn back to you.
Deliver me from the guilt of bloodshed, O
    God,
    you who are God my Savior,
    and my tongue will sing of your
       righteousness.
Open my lips, Lord,
    and my mouth will declare your praise.
You do not delight in sacrifice, or I would
       bring it;
    you do not take pleasure in burnt offerings.
My sacrifice, O God, is a broken spirit;
a broken and contrite heart
you, God, will not despise.

May it please you to prosper Zion,
    to build up the walls of Jerusalem.
Then you will delight in the sacrifices of the
       righteous,
    in burnt offerings offered whole;
    then bulls will be offered on your altar.

When our piano was out of tune, I could still play it. But it sounded off. There was one key that stuck a little, the G one octave up from the middle. The songs weren't as melodious as they could have been. And I knew it was wrong. I could hear it. I'd hit a certain note and physically cringe. Or play a song and shake my head at the first few chords that didn't sound like I'd imagined they should. For months I just let it be out of tune. Awful, right? But eventually I decided it was a priority to have our piano tuned. I couldn't do it myself. It didn't matter how many hours I spent practicing my scales or going over a piece of music, there wasn't anything I could do to make our piano sound better.

I needed an expert. A specialist. An actual piano tuner.

The man who tunes our piano tunes the pianos on the college campus in our town—from the stunning, shiny black grands in the concert halls to the practical wooden uprights in the music majors' practice rooms. He has an assortment of odd-looking tools and some sort of digital screen with red lights that he sets just above the keys while he works. It measures the notes on some quality or other when he strikes a key. He leans in and listens with well-trained ears, then adjusts the inner workings accordingly. It's fascinating to watch. All those strings and tiny felt hammers.

This instrument with 88 keys and approximately 220 strings can be taken from out of tune to perfectly pitched with the turning of screws, the tightening of this and loosening of that. A tuner checks things like temperament and harmonics to allow the piano to make the most beautiful sound it is capable of. Without his tools or skill set or ears I wouldn't even know where to start.

I'm kind of like our piano.

I'm fine. I *can* go about my day without being tuned by Jesus, but I'll be sharp in some areas, flat in others, and off-key. Some parts of my personality will feel a bit sticky. Words will come out differently than I hoped. I'll be jealous of someone. I'll resent something a family member asks me to do. I'll say something snarky about a certain politician. I'll snap at one of my kids. And then I'll feel badly about all of the above. I'll scold myself for not being more rooted in my identity in Christ and for being selfish and judgmental.

I'll try again the next day to be better, but until I get tuned by the Lord, I'll continue to be flat and sharp and off-key. It won't matter how much I promise myself that I'll do better. It doesn't matter how hard I try. I'll scroll through social media and pause and get that twang in my heart that makes me think, Why? Why are so many people following her? What's her secret sauce? Should I post content similar to hers?

Or one of my kids will be grumpy and I'll be tired. And my feelings will get hurt that they aren't reciprocating the love and attention I'm trying to give them. And instead of asking them what's wrong, in my hurt condition I'll subconsciously lash out and decide now would be a great time to remind them of chores they need to do, complete with a sassy tone implying I'm disappointed they haven't already done them. Ugh!

I feel awful because I've slipped, because I'm doing the things I don't want to do. Do you ever feel this way too? The apostle Paul did. He says in Romans 7:15, "I don't really understand myself, for I want to do what is right, but I don't do it. Instead, I do what I hate" (NLT).

Thankfully, we don't need a case full of tools or any special training to tweak our souls. Because even if we had them, we still couldn't do it by ourselves. If I had my piano tuner's tools, I wouldn't know what to do with them. I need to call him and ask him to tune our piano for me. The same is true with my heart and God. I need to call out to God and ask for His help.

King David knew this too. He was no stranger to sin. David messed up big-time when he saw his friend's wife taking a bath. Not only did David peek at this married woman in the tub but then he ordered messengers to bring her to him. She had no choice but to come to the king's quarters as commanded. A woman would have had to comply with the king's requests. He slept with her and Bathsheba became pregnant. As if this weren't bad enough, David covered up the whole thing. He made sure Bathsheba's husband, Uriah, was killed in battle. Uriah could have gotten his wife pregnant before he died, right? Who would ever know? (See 2 Samuel 11–12.)

David thought another man's wife was one hot item, looked when he knew he shouldn't, had sex with her, got her pregnant, and killed her husband to erase the evidence. But David also loved God.

David's sin disgusts us. And it disgusted David. My sin disgusts me. David felt ashamed and so out of tune and knew that he couldn't tune himself—but that there was One who could. After being confronted by the prophet Nathan about what he had done, David wrote this song:

> Have mercy on me, O God,
>   according to your unfailing love;
> according to your great compassion
>   blot out my transgressions.
> Wash away all my iniquity
>   and cleanse me from my sin. (Psalm
>   51:1–2)

David begged God for forgiveness. This is step one. Asking God for forgiveness is important and such a relief. And just like I appreciate it when people tell me they're sorry, God also likes it when we tell Him we're sorry.

There's comfort in knowing that King David, who was a man after God's own heart (1 Samuel 13:14), also stumbled. Big-time. And that Paul, who wrote a good chunk of the New Testament, messed up over and over too. We're not alone. But there's even more comfort in the fact that not only *can* God help us—He *wants* to. Our God is in the restoration business. He's great at it, and it delights Him to make His children whole, complete, loved, and good.

As I was saying earlier, I can feel bad about my behavior, I can say I'm sorry, and I do, but I still stumble at trying to change my ways if I don't also do step two of the tuning process. King David knew all about step two and wrote about it in Psalm 51:

> Create in me a pure heart, O God,
>   and renew a steadfast spirit within me.
> Do not cast me from your presence
>   or take your Holy Spirit from me.
> Restore to me the joy of your salvation
>   and grant me a willing spirit, to sustain
> me. (vv. 10–12)

Step two involves asking God to change us. To make our hearts pure, to renew, restore, and sustain us. God can do all this! It's the most beautiful thing. We are a hot mess. We can't fix ourselves. And . . . we don't have to! Jesus not only has all the tools to make our songs sound sweet but He loves tuning our hearts and souls until they are in perfect pitch with Him. This is amazing grace!

As Paul puts it, "But [God] said to me, 'My grace is sufficient for you, for my power is made perfect in weakness'" (2 Corinthians 12:9).

We don't need more willpower or a stronger resolve; we need Jesus. And He will help us grow these things. His grace is all we need.

Does this mean we ask God to change us but then decide to do whatever we want? Scream at our families, hide behind our screens, give in to our vices, pick up old addictions?

Absolutely not! Because if we're truly sorry and honestly want God to change us, why would we do any of that?

It means that if there is something, as with Paul or David, that we do but wish we didn't, if there is something in our lives that sounds flat or sharp and we want it to sound melodious, we can take it to Jesus. We can first apologize, acknowledging we're off-key. And second, we can ask Him, the one who created music, the one who created us, to change, restore, and sustain us.

Jesus will lean in and listen to our hearts. He'll stretch this and tighten that. And, sure, that's uncomfortable sometimes—facing our sin, trying new, healthier ways to tackle our shame or anger or loneliness. Learning and adapting to God's ways. We feel the tension on our strings as Jesus tunes us. But it's so worth it. It's incredible how beautiful the music of my life is when I ask Jesus to fine-tune me. How little her large number of followers or them being grumpy bothers me. How I can see people better through His eyes. How I can see myself better through Christ's eyes. How I'm less interested in sinful behavior that used to tempt me.

Just like my piano will get out of tune again and I'll need to call back our tuner, I'll get out of tune again too. Christ's forgiveness is one and done. He's already forgiven us for all our sins and all the ways we'll stumble in the future—but staying in tune with Him is still a daily process.

As Hudson Taylor, a missionary to China, said, "Do not have your concert *first*, and then tune your instruments *afterwards*. Begin the day with the Word of God and prayer, and get first of all into harmony with Him."[10]

Getting into harmony with Jesus before we start our days is a game changer. It requires setting aside a few minutes of quiet and being willing to not just come to God with a list of concerns, although that's totally fine to do, but also take a moment or two or ten to listen to His responses.

For me, sharing with Him the things He already knows I messed up yesterday is a relief—to get them off my chest and out in the open. To let His healing love rush over the places where I've scratched and dented myself and others. To allow the Master Tuner to reveal to me in prayer why something upset me, why I couldn't let go of that. To listen as He instructs me how I could apologize or set boundaries or reach out to someone today. And then I ask God again to renew a steadfast spirit within me. I fully mean it when I ask, because I know how melodious it is to be in tune with Him. And then an indescribable peace sinks into my bones. I have a sudden urge to exhale and let His beautiful melody of love, acceptance, and grace play in perfect tune over my heart.

RESTORE

What do you need fine-tuned in your heart?

Take this thing and begin with step one: tell Jesus about it and say you're sorry. Step two: ask Jesus to create in you a pure heart.

Write or print out Psalm 51:10: "Create in me a pure heart, O God, and renew a steadfast spirit within me." Put this on your bathroom mirror so in the morning you'll remember to ask God to help you with whatever you're struggling with. And in the evening, thank God for the ways He kept you in tune. If you went a little off-key, remember this isn't all up to you. Ask Jesus again to tune your heart to His.

17

FONDUE, FEAR, AND PHONE CALLS

Psalm 61

Hear my cry, O God;
*   listen to my prayer.*

From the ends of the earth I call to you,
*   I call as my heart grows faint;*
*   lead me to the rock that is higher than I.*
For you have been my refuge,
*   a strong tower against the foe.*

I long to dwell in your tent forever
*   and take refuge in the shelter of your*
*   wings.*
For you, God, have heard my vows;
*   you have given me the heritage of those*
*   who fear your name.*

Increase the days of the king's life,
*   his years for many generations.*
May he be enthroned in God's presence
*   forever;*
*   appoint your love and faithfulness to pro-*
*   tect him.*

Then I will ever sing in praise of your name
*   and fulfill my vows day after day.*

Archie, who looked about fifty years too young for his name, glided behind the bar. In one swoop he wiped down a spot on the counter, refilled a glass of chardonnay for a customer, grabbed two menus, and sashayed over to the round high-topped table in the corner. He knew the customers sitting there, joked with them, and asked if he could get them their usual drinks.

My husband and I were enjoying watching Archie work from our perch at the smooth marble-topped bar, where we could dine from the bar menu much more economically than the dinner menu. I dipped a hunk of baguette in the cheese fondue we'd ordered as an appetizer and savored every gooey drop.

My husband, handsome in his black sweater, tap-tapped his Fitbit.

"You okay?" I mumbled with my mouth full of warm, cheesy deliciousness.

He raised his eyebrows and tilted his head. "I got a text. But it just says 'Dad.' And then there's a second one. 'Dad.'"

I checked my phone to see if our child who'd messaged Brett had sent me anything. We try to avoid our devices while on a date, but Brett and I were out of town, and if our child needed us, we wanted to respond. I *also* had a text from her from a few minutes before: "Mom, I am actually terrified."

"You okay?" I texted but didn't even wait for an answer before I called her. My husband and I were at the beach—just the two of us. My mom was watching the kids, but I knew our youngest had basketball practice that night and my mom would be with him there. The two other kids were out doing their things, leaving our other child home alone.

As her phone went to voice mail, she texted me: "It sounds like someone is on the stairs."

I read it out loud to Brett.

"Do you have Rob and Judi's number?" he asked.

I nodded and called our next-door neighbors.

After only a three-second explanation, Judi reassured me, "Rob and I are on our way over."

I texted our daughter, "I'm going to call. Answer your phone. Rob and Judi are coming to the front door. Answer it. I'll be on the phone in case you need me."

I exhaled, looked at Brett. "I'm going to call her." I inclined my head to the door. "I'll be back. Sorry."

"Go." He nodded.

Brett and I switched from date mode to protect-our-daughter mode in a single heartbeat. We didn't have to think about it. There wasn't any necessary transition. Our child needed us, and we responded immediately.

God does this for us when we call out to Him. Except, of course, He does it way better. It doesn't matter what else is going on in the world; when we cry out, Jesus is there. That's why David belts out in Psalm 61:

> Hear my cry, O God;
>   listen to my prayer.
>
> From the ends of the earth I call to you,
>   I call as my heart grows faint. (vv. 1–2)

Because David knew God would answer. He didn't know what that would mean exactly. But he knew it was better than not calling out to the Lord. The same way our child knew we would answer if she texted us. She didn't know exactly what we could do to help from South Carolina while she was in her bedroom in Ohio, but she knew it would be better than not calling out.

"Are you okay?"

"Mom," she whispered, "I keep hearing banging in the hallway. Like someone's bowling down the stairs. Oh, that's the door. What should I do?"

"Get to the door and let Rob and Judi in," I told her as

I stepped out into the parking lot, a warm, beachy breeze blowing against my face. "Keep me on the phone. Keep talking to me. If anyone is in the house, they'll hear you talking and think someone's with you."

"Okay," she told me in an anxious voice. Then in her friendly voice I heard her answering the door. "Hi."

In Psalm 61 King David basically says, "I don't know what I need, God, but I need you. You've kept me safe in the past. I'm trusting you'll do it again."

> Lead me to the rock that is higher than I.
> For you have been my refuge,
> a strong tower against the foe. (vv. 2–3)

This was our daughter's heart cry too. She didn't know what she needed, but she trusted that Brett and I would somehow be able to get her to a safe spot. Not because she could touch, see, or feel us in that moment, but because we'd kept her safe in the past.

Rob's and Judi's voices were reassuring in the background. I stayed on the line, listening to my daughter explain what she'd heard and to Judi making small talk to comfort and distract her while Rob searched our house.

Calmer now that our neighbors were with our girl, I texted my mom. She replied instantly, telling me she was on her way back to our house. She'd let our son's coach know that she'd return a few minutes after practice ended.

Brett frantically peeked out from the restaurant entrance. I walked toward him. "She's okay. Rob and Judi are there now. I think she just got spooked. But she's all right. Are you okay in there?"

"We're all good. Take your time. Come back whenever you're ready," Brett reassured me in a calm voice. "The house is old and creaky. It can be pretty loud."

I nodded. "Maybe."

"Glad she's okay." He headed back in so Archie wouldn't think we'd dined and ditched.

Meanwhile I stayed on the phone while Rob walked the perimeter of our house. He gave an all clear and kindly invited our daughter over until my mom returned, but she acted brave and said, "No. I'm fine. It was probably nothing."

There had been a lot of details to execute in a matter of minutes. Texting and calling our daughter. Also calling the neighbors and texting my mom. Leaving the restaurant while holding our table. Having Brett do one thing while I did the other. But it's what we do when the people we love need us. If we, as imperfect parents, could and would do all that for our girl, can you imagine how much the perfect, almighty, omnipotent God will do for us, His children, when we call?

Soon she said, "Grandma's here. I'm just going to go back with her to pick up Maguire."

"Okay. You all right?" I asked.

"Yeah. I'm okay. It's dumb."

"It's not dumb. You heard something and you were alone and that's scary. I'm glad you texted. And I'm even more glad that you're okay." Then I added, both because I was incredibly grateful and so my daughter could be reminded of who her protector was, "Thank you, Jesus, for keeping our girl safe."

We never found out what those noises were, but it doesn't matter. Our little (not so little) girl was safe. That's what mattered. It wasn't exactly how I'd have scripted my romantic French dinner date with my husband, but I would do it again a hundred times over. And Brett would be just as helpful, caring, and gracious all those one hundred times. My mom would gladly drive the extra hour round-trip again to ensure our daughter's safety. And our kind neighbors would walk next door to check on our daughter every night of the week if we asked. Because we all care about this girl and her well-being.

If this is what we would all pitch in to do for our daughter on a February evening, don't you think God would do anything in His power—and, oh yeah, He's all-powerful—to care for us in our hour of need? Because we all need protection. Sometimes more profoundly than others. We have times when we don't feel secure. When we long for safe shelter. David expresses this longing in the psalm.

> I long to dwell in your tent forever
>   and take refuge in the shelter of your
>   wings.
> For you, God, have heard my vows. (vv. 4–5)

This episode with our daughter illustrates the truth of this psalm so vividly for me. She craved safety. And God provided it. It doesn't matter what made the noises she heard; it wasn't dumb for our girl to reach out to us, because the reality was that she was scared. People who love us do everything in their power to protect us when we're frightened. Since God loves us perfectly, we can be assured He will always take our texts and calls. He promises to never leave or forsake us (Hebrews 13:5). He's always there with angel armies to protect us. And because He is almighty, that means our God can take on everything that puts us on edge. He's more powerful.

> May [we] reign under God's protection
>   forever.
> May your unfailing love and faithfulness
>   watch over [us].
> Then I will sing praises to your name forever.
>   (Psalm 61:7–8 NLT)

So what are we afraid of?

The unknown? The diagnosis? The confrontation? Failing? Falling?

I invited my girl to come with me on some errands a couple of weeks after this event and made a comment about not wanting her to have to be home alone.

She laughed and said, "I don't mind being home alone. No one is actually afraid of being home alone. What people are afraid of is someone who wasn't invited being there when you *thought* you were alone."

We don't need to invite fear into our lives. In fact, we should slam the door in fear's face. Fear is not of God. And as long as we call out to Jesus, fear has to leave. His perfect love casts out fear (1 John 4:18). That word *casts* comes from the Greek word *ballo*, which means "to throw, let go of," or if you're discussing a fluid, "to pour out." This is what Jesus does with our fear when we turn it over to Him. We can throw it out, pour it down the drain, or simply drop it—because God is our strong tower.

RESTORE

List some things you're afraid of.

List some ways God has protected you in the past. Did He keep you from dating the wrong person? Cancel a trip you really wanted to go on, only to find out something dangerous took place there? Did He protect you from getting the job at that company that went bankrupt a year after your interview?

Look up Psalm 61 in several different translations on a Bible app or a website like biblegateway.com or blueletterbible.org. Write out the translation of verses 2 and 3 that most resonates with you and put it somewhere you'll see it all week. I like the Passion Translation:

> For no matter where I am, even when I'm far
>   from home,
> I will cry out to you for a father's help.
> When I'm feeble and overwhelmed by life,
> guide me into your glory, where I am safe
>   and sheltered. (v. 2)

18

SLIPPERY SLOPE

Psalm 73

Surely God is good to Israel,
  to those who are pure in heart.

But as for me, my feet had almost slipped;
  I had nearly lost my foothold.
For I envied the arrogant
  when I saw the prosperity of the wicked.

They have no struggles;
  their bodies are healthy and strong.
They are free from common human burdens;
  they are not plagued by human ills.
Therefore pride is their necklace;
  they clothe themselves with violence.
From their callous hearts comes iniquity;
  their evil imaginations have no limits.
They scoff, and speak with malice;
  with arrogance they threaten oppression.
Their mouths lay claim to heaven,
  and their tongues take possession of the
    earth.
Therefore their people turn to them
  and drink up waters in abundance.
They say, "How would God know?
  Does the Most High know anything?"

This is what the wicked are like—
always free of care, they go on amassing
wealth.

Surely in vain I have kept my heart pure
and have washed my hands in innocence.
All day long I have been afflicted,
and every morning brings new punishments.

If I had spoken out like that,
I would have betrayed your children.
When I tried to understand all this,
it troubled me deeply
till I entered the sanctuary of God;
then I understood their final destiny.

Surely you place them on slippery ground;
you cast them down to ruin.
How suddenly are they destroyed,
completely swept away by terrors!
They are like a dream when one awakes;
when you arise, Lord,
you will despise them as fantasies.

When my heart was grieved
and my spirit embittered,
I was senseless and ignorant;
I was a brute beast before you.

Yet I am always with you;
you hold me by my right hand.
You guide me with your counsel,
and afterward you will take me into glory.
Whom have I in heaven but you?
And earth has nothing I desire besides you.
My flesh and my heart may fail,
but God is the strength of my heart
and my portion forever.

Those who are far from you will perish;
you destroy all who are unfaithful to you.

But as for me, it is good to be near God.
I have made the Sovereign LORD my
refuge;
I will tell of all your deeds.

After successfully having my first six novels published over a span of seven years, I was dropped by my agent and then went three years without a book deal.

I was frustrated and sad, and my confidence was wrecked. There were days upon days of rejections or radio silence from agents and editors, but every once in a while someone would comment on my blog saying, "I needed this so much today. Thank you!" Or an email from a reader who had just finished one of my novels saying, "This book gave me hope when I felt hopeless."

God was the one speaking to these readers, but it reminded me that when I wrote for Him, He used it. And those random comments kept me going. Until one desperate day, after yet another rejection from a publisher, hot tears streamed down my face as I pleaded with God, "Do you even still want me to do this?"

I felt God telling me, "Write for me. Tell them about me. Not for book deals or publication, but just to let people know who I am."

And so each day I kept walking into my writing nook, sitting down in my white spinny chair with the lavender polka-dot cushion, and carving out hours to write on a consistent basis. I loved the actual process, spending time reading the Bible, researching, playing with stories in my mind, and figuring out how best to tell them. God taught me so much in that season. I wrote a Bible study, a novel, a nonfiction book. They all sat in files on my laptop.

Then one day I got a reply from an editor at a major publisher to whom I'd sent a proposal for my new novel.

She answered my email in one day. Which, for the record, never happens in publishing. She told me she "loved my story" and took it to her board for review.

The next email I received from her said, "Our team loved the story and thinks you're a great writer." But, she continued, their company was really looking for "clean reads" that would appeal to Christians and non-Christians alike. My story was pretty reliant on the main character's faith. Could I change it up a bit to fit their model?

Hmm . . . Could I pull out the overt faith and keep the story? I thought I could. I started editing, and, sure, I could have the main character be moral, stand up for the important things, have hope, but not necessarily say where she got her inner strength or why she thought it was so important to do what was right. It could work.

There's nothing wrong with a clean read, right? I wanted my kids to read clean fiction, and once they hit the young adult shelves there were fewer and fewer choices that fit that bill. I'd been recently frustrated reading a highly acclaimed novel with a brilliant plot when I landed in an explicit sex scene that was unnecessary and inappropriate and made me put the book down, never to find out how the otherwise intriguing story ended.

I could do this. Offer a book I'd be happy for my own kids to read and get the break I'd been looking for, that I'd been praying for.

The editor applauded my revisions, but I started questioning myself. Clean fiction is great. I prefer reading it. I am grateful for both the Christian and non-Christian authors who write it.

But God had specifically asked me, Laura L. Smith, to tell people about *Him*. All my novels to date had been about the real struggles high school and college girls go through (body image, relationships, addictions, etc.) and how the best way to get through those things is a relationship with Jesus. Watering down that message diluted what God had called *me* to write.

But it was a *big* publisher and a giant break after such a long writing drought and so many days down on my knees, plus the editor was delightful.

It was a slippery slope I was treading.

We've all been on one before. That place where it's tempting, so tempting, to be conformed to the world, even though God begs us not to be, because He offers something so much better. Peeking over our classmate's shoulder to compare their answer on question twenty-three. "Innocently" flirting with a married coworker over coffee. Expensing a meal we ate out the day after we returned from our business trip. Watching that raunchy movie everyone's been talking about or indulging in that food or drink that should be off-limits for our health. Everyone else seems just fine doing these things.

Asaph, the author of Psalm 73, understands this slippery slope too well.

> But as for me, my feet had almost slipped;
>   I had nearly lost my foothold.
> For I envied the arrogant
>   when I saw the prosperity of the wicked.
>   (vv. 2–3)

Living in a culture obsessed with sex, money, and power is tricky. It's even trickier when we see the people who are conforming to culture seemingly prosper. They have all the followers, the clout, the prestige, the designer shoes, and, in my case, the big book deals.

And so we rationalize.

That teacher's tests are unfair.

It's only coffee.

What's one more meal on our company's giant bankroll?

If no one else is home, no one will know.

The young adult novels that hit the best-seller lists? Those books are littered with f-bombs and casual sex. A clean novel is so much better. It's a good thing. Right?

Asaph continues in his song about how those prosperous wicked people he's referring to seem not to have any struggles. They're healthy. They're strong (v. 4). Sure, they're prideful, violent, evil, and say nasty things, but everyone looks up to them. They're rich and famous (vv. 4–12).

This social scenario did not come to an end in Asaph's day. Some celebrities and business moguls today with millions of dollars and followers are objectifying themselves or the women in their lives, treating the people around them like dirt, putting power and wealth above relationships, or promoting a party lifestyle that looks glitzy for their pictures. What we don't see is the aftermath. The hangover, the addiction, the loneliness, the high blood pressure, the string of broken romances and hurting hearts. Yet their fans and supporters can't wait to see what that person eats or wears or where they're going next. Plus, people hang on their every word. Maybe it's worth it?

When we're tempted to cross the line—you know, just move our foot over there—beware. We may slip.

Because cheating on one test can lead to cheating on more tests, which can lead to cheating on tax returns.

Getting away with one lie at work or home might make us think that the next time we're in a bad spot we could do it again, and again, until we're deceiving those around us and ourselves on a regular basis.

That flirtation could lead to more encounters that put our marriage or someone else's in jeopardy.

And that one forbidden sip or nibble could lead to a downward spiral. Just like taking Jesus out of one book could lead to taking Him out of other things I write, and things I say, and everyday rhythms in my life. I don't want to end up in those places, but the slopes are slippery.

As the apostle Paul tells the church in Thessalonica, "Hold on to what is good, reject every kind of evil" (1 Thessalonians 5:21–22).

As soon as I'd submitted the revised manuscript, I felt uneasy. I started praying for God's will to be done. For the book to move forward if this was Him answering my prayers for ways to write for Him. Or for the deal to crumble if this was not what He had in mind.

Although the publisher applauded the revisions to my novel, at the last minute the contract was halted by the marketing team who noted my website and social media were all about Jesus, which didn't match the clean, mainstream image they were going for. They were concerned it would confuse and possibly turn off readers. I exhaled audibly and praised Jesus when I got that rejection. Because He had protected me from something He didn't want me to do. That would have been fine, great even, for so many writers but dangerous for me. Jesus does that for us. He doesn't want us to fall.

> You hold me by my right hand.
> You guide me with your counsel,
>   and afterward you will take me into glory.
> Whom have I in heaven but you?
>   And earth has nothing I desire besides you.
>   (vv. 23–25)

I was this close to stumbling and falling hard for a trap of this world. But God had asked me to do something else. And for a couple of weeks, I disobeyed Him. Because my eyes were blurry with the world's definition of success. Because I was desperate. I wanted a book deal. I'm a writer. And I hadn't had a book contract in so long. But that wasn't the kind of book deal I actually wanted, because it wasn't the kind God wanted for me.

I immediately put Jesus back into the pages of the

book, right where He belonged. But today, years later, this novel has never been published. Maybe someday it will. I'd love for you to meet the main character and read her story. But maybe it won't. Maybe the whole reason God had me write that book was so I could learn, down to my very core, what He's called me to write and how important it is to stick to His vision.

Not anyone else's.

No matter what.

Sometimes we want more money, time, or attention, and we're tempted to do something we know we shouldn't to get those things. Maybe something small. Maybe something big. Maybe something that's perfectly fine for those around us.

Some days God steps in and saves us before our toe ever gets close to the line. *Thank you, Jesus.* Other times He tries to redirect and remind us, but we disregard Him. Our eyes are so fixed on the worldly prizes that we dismiss God's promptings. We take our eyes off our true prize and portion. How do we guard ourselves from being hypnotized by those shiny carrots dangling right in front of our faces? The psalmist tells us:

> My flesh and my heart may fail,
>   but God is the strength of my heart
>   and my portion forever. (v. 26)

That's it.

We need to make God the strength of our heart. We need to go to Him daily, ask His advice, beg His forgiveness, and worship Him, reminding ourselves of how good He is. When we do, we reset. We remember what's truly important. It's not fame or fortune. It's the love of our heavenly Father, which we already have.

I got so caught up in the allure of a big book deal that I didn't take time to pray when things were moving forward, not really. I kind of uttered some words, thanked God for the awesome opportunity, and didn't listen to His response. It was when I finally asked Him to be in charge that the door slammed shut and I could see that God was my portion. If the word "portion" isn't doing it for you, "everything I need" or "my inheritance" are also great translations from the original Hebrew.

We can bask in God's love and provision. Let it be what feeds and strengthens us. Go to Him first. And then, instead of slipping, we can find our balance.

—— RESTORE ——

Is there something in this world that is currently or repeatedly tempting you?

How are you trying to keep your footing? How is that working for you?

The best way to resist temptation is to set our heart on the God who is our strength. Make "God is the portion of my heart" your screen saver on your phone. Or write it on a sticky note and put it on the bottle, the remote, the credit card . . . wherever you think it will help you most. Each time you pick up whatever you wrote "God is everything I need" on, make sure you read this truth. Don't tap or swipe or ignore before focusing on the fact that God is what you truly need. When possible, declare it out loud. Let the truth of God sustaining you sink in, so when you're tempted to step into the danger zone, you can keep your feet firm.

19

I'D DO ANYTHING TO GET THERE

Psalm 84

How lovely is your dwelling place,
  LORD Almighty!
My soul yearns, even faints,
  for the courts of the LORD;
my heart and my flesh cry out
  for the living God.
Even the sparrow has found a home,
  and the swallow a nest for herself,
  where she may have her young—
a place near your altar,
  LORD Almighty, my King and my God.
Blessed are those who dwell in your house;
  they are ever praising you.

Blessed are those whose strength is in you,
  whose hearts are set on pilgrimage.
As they pass through the Valley of Baka,
  they make it a place of springs;
  the autumn rains also cover it with pools.
They go from strength to strength,
  till each appears before God in Zion.

Hear my prayer, LORD God Almighty;
  listen to me, God of Jacob.

Look on our shield, O God;
  look with favor on your anointed one.

Better is one day in your courts
  than a thousand elsewhere;
I would rather be a doorkeeper in the house
      of my God
  than dwell in the tents of the wicked.
For the LORD *God is a sun and shield;*
  the LORD *bestows favor and honor;*
no good thing does he withhold
  from those whose walk is blameless.

LORD *Almighty,*
  blessed is the one who trusts in you.

We can smell the salty sea air before we can see it. Even though our family of six has been in the car together for twelve hours, and now we're lugging our baggage up three flights of stairs, there is excitement and anticipation. Our steps are quick, our smiles bursting across our faces. Once inside the door, we know right where to go. We drop bags on the white-tiled floor and set belongings on counters. As soon as our arms are free, we scurry to the screen doors, sliding them open, and step onto the balcony to gaze at the ocean.

We don't live here. But we come here most summers. And to us it feels like home, like a place we would return to every month of every year—if money and time and distance weren't issues. We inhale deeply the brininess of the air. We let the sound of water in motion wash over us. The hours and miles in the van we rented melt off our shoulders. Any exhaustion we felt or bickering we experienced during the road trip seems to dissipate. Our worries fade. We feel invigorated, more alive than we remember feeling in a while.

I believe this is a glimpse of what it's like to be in the presence of God.

In awe. Thrilled. At peace. Able to lay down our burdens. At home.

The psalmist who wrote Psalm 84 felt this. The psalmist knew that being with God is better than being anywhere else—that it's a place you want to rush to, marinate in, savor, and get to as quickly as you can.

> How lovely is your dwelling place,
>   LORD Almighty!
> My soul yearns, even faints,
>   for the courts of the LORD;
> my heart and my flesh cry out
>   for the living God. (vv. 1–2)

Do you have a place like this? A place you long for? That makes you feel closer to the living God, the things He's created, the life He's designed for you?

Maybe it's going back to your parents' house for the holidays, walking in the door and smelling the cinnamon of an apple pie bubbling over its flaky crust in the oven, holding hands at the dinner table, your dad praying over the meal in his deep baritone, and you kind of get that knot in your throat and feel nostalgic for the more innocent, less complicated days of your childhood, for this place where you always feel safe and known. Even though your daily struggles are still real, in the moment they feel more manageable, lighter.

Or maybe you have a friend's apartment where every time you enter it your shoulders relax, you're able to share what's been on your mind, and you laugh more than you have in days. She always has a steaming mug of peppermint tea laced with honey waiting for you. There's something about the way the light comes in through that giant window. But it's not just that she's made the space inviting; it's her warm smile, the way she listens, the way it's so easy to talk with her about your struggles and Jesus and how He's moving in your life. You can't wait to walk through her door, slide off your shoes, tuck your feet under the fuzzy gray throw folded across her couch, be seen and heard for who you truly are, no faking, no pretenses.

I believe these oases are sneak peeks of God's kingdom here on earth. Portals to what it feels like to be fully loved, fully ourselves, safe, joyful, at ease. I believe this is true because it sounds so much like what Jesus tells us "getting away with Him" looks and feels like.

> Are you tired? Worn out? Burned out on religion? Come to me. Get away with me and you'll recover your life. I'll show you how to take a real rest. Walk with me and work with me—watch how I do it. Learn the unforced rhythms of grace. I won't lay anything heavy or ill-fitting on you. Keep company with me and you'll learn to live freely and lightly. (Matthew 11:28–30 MSG)

A real rest.
Unforced rhythms of grace.
Nothing heavy or ill-fitting.
Yes, please.

Note that Jesus doesn't say we're going to swing on hammocks all day. Although I don't think He'd mind if we took an afternoon siesta on one. He says, "Walk with me and work with me." Walk? Like exercise? Work? Wait—there's work involved in bliss?

Of course. But it's walking that moves us forward, like grinding through the classes necessary to get certified. And it's good work, sometimes exhausting work, but the kind we know truly matters, like caring for a child with special needs.

Although I love writing, sometimes it's laborious.

Trying to convey an idea I know in my soul into words for others to grasp. Doing it within set guidelines, word counts, and timelines. Yet at the beach my brain feels free. Surrounded by warm breezes and rhythmic waves, my creativity flows. I almost always get ideas for new chapters, articles, and books. Finding new writing material doesn't feel like work in my Hilton Head habitat. It's exciting and invigorating.

And tearing bread into bite-size chunks for the Thanksgiving stuffing while my mom mixes the filling for a pecan pie? This feels completely different than trying to meal plan for six people, three with food allergies, all with different tastes and busy evening schedules on a daily basis. Cooking in the kitchen with my sweet mama at the holidays, talking and laughing feels like a treat. That's not ill-fitting work. It fits nicely, thank you very much. This is a peek at heaven. Living free and light. And not free in the sense that we have no accountability but that the things we're responsible for feel good and right and satisfying.

These special places, these glimpses of the kingdom of heaven, are like the scenes in movies where the music is playing and you see a montage of the character moving forward, overcoming, becoming who they were always meant to be.

How do we find these places that help us sense God's kingdom, get back to them, and replicate them when we can't get away, when our calendars are jammed, when our workload is demanding, when our heart aches for someone we mourn, or when we take care of someone who needs constant attention?

We have to be intentional. We need to be alert to these spaces where we hear God more clearly, where we're more in tune to the kind of life Jesus talks about—one where there is walking and working, where the rhythms are unforced and filled with grace. If these destinations help us connect with God and the kingdom life He has for us, then we can use them to "seek first his kingdom and his righteousness" (Matthew 6:33). If we can identify a special place that helps us feel the peace God offers more tangibly, we should try to get back to it and seek God's will, refreshment, strength, and joy while we're there.

Psalm 84 explains,

> What joy for those whose strength comes
> from the LORD,
> who have set their minds on a pilgrimage
> to Jerusalem.
> When they walk through the Valley of
> Weeping,
> it will become a place of refreshing springs.
> The autumn rains will clothe it with
> blessings.
> They will continue to grow stronger,
> and each of them will appear before God
> in Jerusalem. (vv. 5–7 NLT)

That makes sense, right? If we set our minds on finding the places where we're more in tune with God, we'll become refreshed, blessed, and grow stronger. Because we're on a pilgrimage to find our God and the life He offers us.

And, yes, this might seem like me rationalizing some bonus beach vacations, which is not a bad idea, but actually I'm encouraging all of us to *seek the places where we feel or understand God better.*

We can take inventory of what it is about these spaces that brings us back to the loving arms of God and helps us lay down our defenses, be ourselves, and receive the joy He offers.

Then we can search for spaces with similar characteristics in our typical habitats so we can be reminded of kingdom living more often and more fully experience it in our everyday routines.

For me the ocean is bliss. But why?

The fresher air, God's beautiful, untamed creation. No screens and the quieter schedule. Long stretches to think and pray and listen. I can't re-create the ocean in Ohio, but there are lovely wooded trails near my house where I can go on quiet walks and breathe in the smell of wildflowers in the summer and the sweetness of leaves in the fall. There's nothing human-made except the crushed stone path weaving between the trees. It's all God-made, and that's part of the allure of the beach too. I don't hear the rush of waves in the woods, but I do hear the trickle of water dancing along the streambed. I marvel at creation. And in the quiet, away from technology, I think and pray and listen to God. It's not Hilton Head, but guess what? I find God here. I feel Him. I hear Him.

If going home for the holidays is your sweet spot, how do you incorporate that peace and contentment into busy days of volunteering, working your part-time job, and throwing a meal together before an evening meeting on a Thursday? What is it about the holidays that you treasure? Being surrounded by people you love? Holding hands, that tender human contact and connection while praying? The pine-scented candle burning and Christmas carols playing, which wake up your senses dulled from staring at your laptop or television?

Life might be hurried, but why not try to capture that feeling throughout the year? Jesus tells us how valuable His kingdom is—why we should seek it out: "Again, the kingdom of heaven is like a merchant looking for fine pearls. When he found one of great value, he went away and sold everything he had and bought it" (Matthew 13:45–46). You, too, can intentionally seek for the fine pearls of kingdom living. Why not schedule regular dinners with your local community, whether that's your family, roomies, neighbors, or small group from church? Play some worship music, light a vanilla candle, and let its soft light flicker and revive your awareness to be present. Ask everyone to hold hands and take turns praying. It doesn't make a Sunday in September feel like Christmas, but it reminds us the goodness of God is available to us all.

My soul yearns for these kinds of spaces.

Yours?

Places where we smile and sway. Where the work is gratifying. Places where God's voice is louder, His presence more tangible.

> Better is one day in your courts
> than a thousand elsewhere. (v. 10)

Jesus promises to be with us wherever we go (Matthew 28:20). He lives inside of every Christian (Romans 8:10–11). But in this broken world sometimes that's hard to remember. We forget. God wants us to remember that He is present with us always.

In *Pirates of the Caribbean*, Jack Sparrow has a compass that leads him to his heart's desire. In *Beauty and the Beast*, the Beast gives Belle a mirror that allows her to see whatever she most wants to see. Why do storytellers think we'll buy into these charmed objects?

Because all of us long to see our heart's desire.

And when our heart's desire is Jesus, the thing we most long to see is Him.

I believe Christ gives us not compasses or mirrors but special places and people as portals to see more of Him in our mixed-up, topsy-turvy world. In our special settings, cities, communities, or landscapes we catch glimpses of how much our Savior loves us, of the peace and joy He offers, of how satisfying work can be, of a free life.

Jesus invites us into this kingdom living today. His door is open. The logs are crackling in the fireplace, the tunes already playing, and He has a spread of all our favorite foods laid out. He has some intriguing, satisfying work for us to do. He'll engage us in stimulating conversations and listen to everything we want to say. There is joy and peace and grace there.

We don't have to drive twelve hours to get there. We don't have to wait until Christmas. All we have to do is seek Him, walk with Him, get away with Him.

This free and light life is waiting. It's better than anywhere else. It feels like home. And I can't wait to get back.

———— RESTORE ————

Close your eyes and imagine your favorite space—the place where you feel most at home, most real, most known, most full of joy. Who is there with you? What does it smell like? What does it sound like? How do you feel God there?

What are some things in that place that you could replicate in your everyday life?

Tell Jesus you're seeking Him, that you're interested in living in His unforced rhythms of grace. Ask Him how to find Him in the busy, mundane, crazy, stressful, sad, boring, painful, or exhausting days. Ask Him to show you how to live more freely and lightly with Him.

20

COUNTING THE DAYS

Psalm 90

Lord, you have been our dwelling place
  throughout all generations.
Before the mountains were born
  or you brought forth the whole world,
  from everlasting to everlasting you are
    God.

You turn people back to dust,
  saying, "Return to dust, you mortals."
A thousand years in your sight
  are like a day that has just gone by,
  or like a watch in the night.
Yet you sweep people away in the sleep of
    death—
  they are like the new grass of the morning:
In the morning it springs up new,
  but by evening it is dry and withered.

We are consumed by your anger
  and terrified by your indignation.
You have set our iniquities before you,
  our secret sins in the light of your presence.
All our days pass away under your wrath;
  we finish our years with a moan.
Our days may come to seventy years,
  or eighty, if our strength endures;

*yet the best of them are but trouble and
    sorrow,
for they quickly pass, and we fly away.
If only we knew the power of your anger!
    Your wrath is as great as the fear that is
    your due.
Teach us to number our days,
    that we may gain a heart of wisdom.*

*Relent, Lord! How long will it be?
    Have compassion on your servants.
Satisfy us in the morning with your unfailing
    love,
    that we may sing for joy and be glad all
    our days.
Make us glad for as many days as you have
    afflicted us,
    for as many years as we have seen trouble.
May your deeds be shown to your servants,
    your splendor to their children.*

*May the favor of the Lord our God rest on us;
    establish the work of our hands for us—
    yes, establish the work of our hands.*

When our oldest was two and a half and I was pregnant with our second child, my husband moved to Ohio while I still lived in Atlanta.

We didn't want to be apart. But Brett's new work situation required him to be in Ohio, and we hadn't sold our house in Atlanta yet or found a new one in the Buckeye State. For three months, Brett spent stretches working in the Midwest and then moments in the South with me and Maddie. And in between, for days on end, it was just me, my tiny toddler, and all our belongings that needed to be packed into boxes.

I adored spending time with my little girl, but it was hard. My pregnant body was cumbersome and tired. I missed my husband. Maddie was curious and wanted to get out every toy I'd put away, touch and play with every pot, pan, or pillow in our entire home, and I was trying to keep our house spotless for prospective buyers. A typical day began with Maddie waking up at six thirty. A realtor would call, maybe at eleven thirty, saying she was going to be showing our house between noon and four. I then executed a frenzied cleanup, exit, and on-the-fly plan of how to entertain a toddler for four hours during her normal nap time.

I spent every moment of those months with sweet Maddie by my side. Which was adorable when baking brownies or finger-painting. But trickier when showering, cleaning toilets, attempting to exercise, or going to the ob-gyn. I'd talk on the phone with Brett, and he was just as exhausted working crazy hours, trying to fix major problems at work, and being away from us. And although most people have been through much worse (shout-out to single moms—you are amazing humans who deserve all the prizes and chocolate that exist on earth), at the time I was so desperate for a few moments alone or an extra hour of sleep or time with my husband that the words Moses cried out in the wilderness echoed in my heart.

> Relent, LORD! How long will it be?
>   Have compassion on your servants.
> Satisfy us in the morning with your unfailing
>   love,
>   that we may sing for joy and be glad all
>   our days.
> Make us glad for as many days as you have
>   afflicted us. (Psalm 90:13–15)

Some scholars believe Moses most likely wrote this psalm during the time referenced in Numbers 20.[11]

Moses's sister, Miriam, had died. So had his brother, Aaron. The Israelites were complaining, asking, "Why did you bring us up out of Egypt to this terrible place?" (v. 5). Plus, God told Moses he wasn't going to be allowed to enter the promised land because Moses had provided water for the people *his* way instead of following God's instructions. It is one rough chapter. Moses definitely had reasons to cry out to the Lord, to beg for compassion.

My days in Atlanta were nothing in comparison. But they were l-o-n-g. And I felt crummy. And when I got Maddie safely tucked into her crib at night, I was on a mission—wrapping dishes in newspaper, stacking books in boxes, and tossing things we no longer needed into garbage bags to pitch or donate. When I finally went to bed, I crawled under the covers, fatigued and alone. And I found myself asking, "How long?"

Have you asked God "How long?" before? Are you asking Him that today?

God made us, knows us, and loves us. God wants us to cry out to Him when we are at our low points. Whether that's because we're out of sorts, we're mourning someone we love, we've made a mistake, we're misunderstood, or we've been erroneously blamed. Moses was all of the above. God wants us to talk to Him about everything that's on our hearts and minds. This includes the annoying stuff, hard stuff, ugly stuff, and the stuff we don't really want to talk about.

Moses goes for it in this psalm. He's emotionally and physically spent. He feels alone and unsure of what's next. And Moses challenges God about it. Same for me when I was in Atlanta. And like Moses, I have a choice. You have a choice. How will we handle the hard seasons of waiting? Will we wallow? Will we dread each day? Or will we lean into God's goodness, trust Him with each and every moment, and see what He has in store?

Despite Moses's painful season, he still knew that God

is good. That despite where Moses was and what was going on around him, God never left the throne.

Same for me again. Thank goodness.

> Lord, you have been our dwelling place
> throughout all generations.
> Before the mountains were born
> or you brought forth the whole world,
> from everlasting to everlasting you are
> God. (vv. 1–2)

This holds true for all of us. No matter what kind of wilderness we're in. It's not easy to praise God in the midst of pain, fear, uncertainty, or exhaustion. But it is effective. Because when we start to praise God, it reminds us that someone cares. That someone sees the ache in our soul and the weariness in our bones and has all the time in the world to listen as we pour out our hearts. Praising God in our deserts creates a shift in our souls. We become more aware of who God truly is, of His steadfast faithfulness from everlasting to everlasting. When we seek His love, it satisfies our inner longings (v. 14). We find security in the fact that God is our dwelling place— our home (v. 1). And our eyes begin to open to God's goodness around us. We might even sing for joy (v. 14).

"Teach us to number our days," Moses begs God, "that we may gain a heart of wisdom" (v. 12).

I began to feel it. Sure, I counted the days on my fingers until Brett would come home for a visit, or until Maddie and I would actually move to Ohio and we could all be together, but I also began to treasure the days, the present I was living. To learn from them. To keep my eyes open to what God was doing in them. Because each and every day God grants us is priceless. As C. S. Lewis says in *The Screwtape Letters*, "The Present is all lit up with eternal rays."[12]

Are we basking in those eternal rays or trying to hurry through our current situations? Because when we stop to savor where we are, right now, today, we get glimpses of heaven and, with them, reminders of God's love and faithfulness.

Maddie and I went on countless adventures to play-grounds, the carousel at the mall, and story times at a magical place called Hobbit Hall that was an old house renovated into a kid's bookstore, complete with cozy nooks to read with your kiddo, toddler-friendly crafts, and a goldfish pond out front. We snuggled and giggled and ate blueberry bagels smeared with cream cheese and sprinkled with cinnamon for dinner. It was Maddie's favorite meal, took almost zero prep, and was one of the few things I could stomach. When else in my life as a wife and mom could I get away with having blueberry bagels for dinner? Maddie and I would make up silly songs and sing them to Brett when he came for visits. And the sight of my husband's blue eyes when he walked in the front door for a weekend or the feel of his arms holding me tight made my heart flutter like when we were first dating.

I have such vivid recollections of those months. My brain knows I was achy and exhausted and lonely at the time, but as I look back it's hard for me to really put those feelings with those days. Because when I tap into those memories, I hear my daughter's laughter as a caterpillar tickles her palm and picture her delighting in the illustrations as we turned the pages of *If You Give a Mouse a Cookie*. Each day I was grateful and tangibly felt joy.

All our days are worth savoring. God is with us in *all* of them. On the days we're expectantly counting down to a wedding or party. On the days we're crossing off squares on the calendar until Christmas break or the cast comes off or the chemo is over or our paper is turned in.

On the days we're watching the clock until we find out if we got into the program or until the shop is open or until we can get our car back from the mechanic. Let's not rush these days with the goal of just getting through. Instead, let's savor them. Learn from them. Seek God in them. All of them. Amen?

———— RESTORE ————

Is there anything in your life you're counting down to?

As you wait for that day to get here, why not seek God daily?

1. Tell God how you feel about it—whether that's freaked out or thrilled or anything in between.

2. Thank God for all the ways He's been there for you in the past.

3. Take a deep breath in and out to orient yourself to this present moment. Look around and see how God is blessing you right here, right now. Thank Him for that too.

21

ICY ROADS

Psalm 91

Whoever dwells in the shelter of the Most
*   High*
* will rest in the shadow of the Almighty.*
I will say of the LORD, *"He is my refuge and*
*   my fortress,*
* my God, in whom I trust."*

Surely he will save you
* from the fowler's snare*
* and from the deadly pestilence.*
He will cover you with his feathers,
* and under his wings you will find refuge;*
* his faithfulness will be your shield and*
*   rampart.*
You will not fear the terror of night,
* nor the arrow that flies by day,*
nor the pestilence that stalks in the darkness,
* nor the plague that destroys at midday.*
A thousand may fall at your side,
* ten thousand at your right hand,*
* but it will not come near you.*
You will only observe with your eyes
* and see the punishment of the wicked.*

If you say, "The LORD *is my refuge,"*
* and you make the Most High your dwelling,*
no harm will overtake you,

no disaster will come near your tent.
For he will command his angels concerning
you
to guard you in all your ways;
they will lift you up in their hands,
so that you will not strike your foot
against a stone.
You will tread on the lion and the cobra;
you will trample the great lion and the
serpent.

"Because he loves me," says the LORD, "I will
rescue him;
I will protect him, for he acknowledges my
name.
He will call on me, and I will answer him;
I will be with him in trouble,
I will deliver him and honor him.
With long life I will satisfy him
and show him my salvation."

One minute we were driving along—the next we were slipping, sliding, and spinning across three lanes of traffic on the snowy highway. It was early Christmas morning, and we were headed to Atlanta to celebrate with my family. Our four-year-old and one-year-old were buckled in their car seats behind us. But as our car careened across I-75 and I watched cars driving straight toward us, I wasn't thinking about mistletoe or holly or angels or baby Jesus. I wasn't thinking about anything except crying out to the Lord. Everything was out of my control—my husband's safety, my safety, the safety of our two precious babies, our car, the other cars and their passengers. I don't know if any words formed in my brain, but I know my heart cried out—*Jesus! Help us!*

Our Nissan zoomed at an uncontrollable speed to the

guardrail at the right side of the freeway, bounced against it like a pinball, and went flying back across the freeway, cars and semis still speeding toward us at over fifty-five miles per hour. I saw the rail on the left side of the road as if it were running toward us, too fast. Way too fast. And we were still spinning. With a thick throat, I shouted out, "I love you!" to Brett, Maddie, and Max. Because it's what I wanted them to know. It's what I wanted them to remember. And I didn't have the time or the wherewithal to say anything else.

All these thoughts flashed through my head in an instant. It's taken me longer to type out this scene than it took in real time. As our car collided with the rail, I squeezed Brett's arm.

And then our car miraculously stopped.

It shouldn't have.

We were going too fast.

The rail was only a couple of feet tall—not thick enough or tall enough to stop the force of our 3,500-pound car. But the tail end of our car hit that rail, and somehow we stayed in place. There was a quiet that surrounded us. In my memory everything is black and white and gray, void of color.

I looked at Brett, then back at the kids. Neither of them was crying. Why weren't they crying?

"You guys okay? Maddie? Max?"

Maddie nodded, her sapphire-blue eyes wide. Max looked serious; his brow furrowed.

"How did we . . . ?"

"I don't know," Brett answered. "My whole life flashed before my eyes."

"How did none of those cars hit us?" I asked.

"I don't know. They were headed right at us. I couldn't stop. We hit an ice patch and we were out of control."

"How did we stop?"

"I don't know," he answered again. "We shouldn't have."

Brett got out of the car and looked it over. It was banged up but drivable. We sat for a few moments, allowing our hearts to slow from rapid-fire to a normal rhythm, for our adrenaline to stop coursing. Then Brett turned the car around, eased back into traffic, got off at the first exit, and pulled into the parking lot of the most welcoming Waffle House we'd ever seen.

The words of Psalm 91 are a perfect narration of our adventure.

> I will say of the LORD, "He is my refuge and
>   my fortress,
>   my God, in whom I trust."
>
> Surely he will save you
>   from the fowler's snare
>   and from the deadly pestilence.
> He will cover you with his feathers,
>   and under his wings you will find refuge;
>   his faithfulness will be your shield and
>   rampart. (vv. 2–4)

God saved us that day.

We could have been killed countless times. But by His grace, through His protection, not one car hit us either the first time we slid across several lanes of traffic or the second, after we'd bounced off the rail. How did we bounce? The rail was made of metal, not rubber. We didn't die from the impact of plunging into the first rail or the second. We could still drive our car home. How? It is inexplicable in human terms or probabilities.

But as the psalmist explains, on that day we could proclaim,

> No harm will overtake you,
>   no disaster will come near your tent [or
>   Nissan].

> For he will command his angels concerning
>   you
> to guard you in all your ways;
> they will lift you up in their hands,
>   so that you will not strike your foot
>   against a stone. (vv. 10–12)

Have you ever had your life flash before your eyes? Ever been saved inexplicably? Missed another car by a whisker? Had the doctor say, "There was something on the initial lab work, but now we don't see anything"? Had someone perform the Heimlich maneuver on you? Or CPR? Did your smoke alarm go off in time for you to put out a fire or escape its flames? Did someone jump in the pool or lake after you when you went out too deep or didn't know how to swim? Has someone whisked away an almond-filled dessert that was set down in front of you because they knew you have a nut allergy?

Have you thanked God for saving you on that day?

Have you thanked Him since then?

I'm not trying to be insensitive to the fact that horrific accidents take place. Teens lose their lives in car crashes. Rescue workers forfeit their lives to save others. Natural disasters wreak havoc and destroy buildings and humanity in their path. These things are devastating. And a reality in this broken world. But God loves all His people. He fights for all of us to know Him, to feel His love and accept His grace. And the instant our heart stops beating here on earth, our good, good Father ushers all who accept His love gently to heaven, where they will live eternally without pain or suffering, steeped in joy (Revelation 21:4). It's still shattering to those left behind. And I have no idea how God decides when it's time for us to come home to Him.

But I do know that God loves each and every one of us, and that He is a rescuer! Don't take my word for it. God says so himself.

"Because he loves me," says the LORD, "I will
    rescue him;
  I will protect him, for he acknowledges my
    name.
He will call on me, and I will answer him;
  I will be with him in trouble,
  I will deliver him and honor him." (Psalm
    91:14–15)

Paul starts out his letter to the Galatians with a proclamation that Jesus's sacrifice on the cross *rescues* us from our sins. Paul also relates to the church in Corinth how God *rescued* him and those traveling with him from dangers in Asia Minor:

Grace and peace to you from God our Father and the Lord Jesus Christ, who gave himself for our sins to *rescue* us from the present evil age, according to the will of our God and Father. (Galatians 1:3–4, emphasis added)

And he did it, *rescued* us from certain doom. And he'll do it again, *rescuing* us as many times as we need *rescuing*. You and your prayers are part of the *rescue* operation. (2 Corinthians 1:10–11 MSG, emphasis added)

We'll never understand all the ways God protects us. Probably never realize all the times He has rescued us. Maybe one day when we're in heaven God will take us aside and explain how when someone we loved was taken from us before we felt capable of losing them, it actually rescued them and others from something we could have never predicted with our limited vision. Maybe that's something only the Almighty can get His mind around. But I believe Jesus when He says He'll protect us. Paul told the Corinthians, "He'll do it again, rescuing us as many times as we need rescuing." God can rescue us from our trials too. I've seen the Lord do it time and time again. That bitter cold Christmas morning on I-75 was just one of the more vivid examples.

Our family calmed our anxious hearts with buttery waffles drowned in sweet, sticky syrup, steaming mugs of coffee for the grown-ups, chocolate milks for the kiddos, and hash browns—scattered, smothered, covered, and diced, thank you very much. We knew we couldn't continue our drive to Atlanta in these conditions. So after breakfast we called my family and gave them the bad news that we wouldn't be there for Christmas. All we wanted to do was snap our fingers and be safe in our own warm house by our tree. We still had to drive two hours north to get back home. That seemed safer than driving six more hours south. But those were two very long, slow, shaky hours.

Fast-forward to the present. My daughter Maddie has loved on and given dignity to so many people through the Best Buddies program at her college and her internship with Special Olympics. I watch my son Max leading worship on his campus, both in church and in small groups. My husband encourages and challenges students at the public university where he teaches to integrate their faith into all aspects of their lives, specifically their business endeavors. I see so clearly that God had important work for all of them to do, and that because He covered us with "his feathers . . . under his wings" on that Christmas long ago, my family members are making an impact on this world—on God's kingdom.

We'll face more hardships. This world is a broken place. But I've witnessed the miraculous power of God's rescue. And I'm holding on to that memory, so I won't forget who our God is and what He's capable of. That we are alive today is a miracle. And I am confident that when I call on Jesus, He will answer me. Not always as I expect or even want to hear. But He will be with me in trouble. He will deliver me. He'll do the same for you. As many times as we need rescuing.

─── RESTORE ───

Have you had a moment where you were close to dying, but someone or something intervened?

If so, take some time to thank God for His provision in that time. Read Psalm 91 out loud, then ask God to help you hold onto that memory so you can trust Him more.

If not, ask your friends, small group, parents, or co-workers to relay their stories to you. Read Psalm 91 out loud and ask God to grow your trust in Him. Thank Him for being a rescuer.

22

FROG CONCERT

Psalm 96

Sing to the LORD a new song;
sing to the LORD, all the earth.
Sing to the LORD, praise his name;
proclaim his salvation day after day.
Declare his glory among the nations,
his marvelous deeds among all peoples.

For great is the LORD and most worthy of
praise;
he is to be feared above all gods.
For all the gods of the nations are idols,
but the LORD made the heavens.
Splendor and majesty are before him;
strength and glory are in his sanctuary.

Ascribe to the LORD, all you families of
nations,
ascribe to the LORD glory and strength.
Ascribe to the LORD the glory due his name;
bring an offering and come into his courts.
Worship the LORD in the splendor of his
holiness;
tremble before him, all the earth.
Say among the nations, "The LORD reigns."
The world is firmly established, it cannot
be moved;
he will judge the peoples with equity.

Let the heavens rejoice, let the earth be glad;
let the sea resound, and all that is in it.
Let the fields be jubilant, and everything in
them;
let all the trees of the forest sing for joy.
Let all creation rejoice before the LORD, for
he comes,
he comes to judge the earth.
He will judge the world in righteousness
and the peoples in his faithfulness.

This is the manor house. You are in the moat house. Your neighbors are the ducks, and there may be a frog concert in the evening." Jacques, looking every bit his part as our French host, complete with ascot, gave our family this welcome speech when we rented a couple of rooms in his moat house (way cheaper than a hotel), which had been occupied by the Germans during World War II.

It was honestly like out of a movie. The Manoir du Quesnay is a sprawling property in Normandy, France, with spotted cows, towers covered in ivy, and spiral staircases constructed of stone. It's situated at the end of a long dirt lane off a tiny country road dotted with similar gray stone manor houses and cows, ten minutes from a fishing village in the French countryside. The floors are slabs of slate, worn and uneven after over six hundred years of wear and tear. The main room has an enormous fireplace used to warm the building prior to the invention of heaters, and the walls are covered in thick tapestries in attempts to hold some of that heat in.

True to Jacques's word, as we brushed our teeth in the pink porcelain bathroom that evening, we heard the frogs warming up their vocal cords and then bursting into high-pitched chirrups for their nightly performance.

Not to be outdone, the next morning the ducks glided across the surface of the pond situated next to the moat house, quacking their hearts out as we climbed into our rented silver van to tour the historic D-Day sites of Omaha and Utah Beaches.

Maybe those ducks and frogs were still singing about D-Day and how the Allied forces freed France from the Nazi regime, how this very building was reclaimed by its rightful owners after being forcibly taken and occupied by the enemy decades ago. Maybe they were just singing because they lived on a gorgeous piece of land in France. I would.

We don't have frogs or ducks at our house, but we do get a cricket concert most summer evenings on our screened porch and beautiful birdsongs trilling through the trees in the springtime. When I stop to listen to these symphonies in nature they always make me smile. Their songs cut through my to-do lists and concerns. They take me to a place that's simpler and sweeter, where I can just enjoy the melody. Where I can just be.

There's something about singing in general that changes our mood, helps us express our emotions, makes us feel alive. And when we sing to the Lord—it's invigorating!

King David wrote Psalm 96 and instructs all of creation to sing out loud. He begins in verse 1, "Sing to the LORD a new song; sing to the LORD, all the earth."

He continues in verses 11 through 13:

> Let the sea resound, and all that is in it.
> Let the fields be jubilant, and everything in
>   them;
>   let all the trees of the forest sing for joy.
> Let all creation rejoice before the LORD.

I sing when I'm happy and also when I'm slaphappy. I sing to celebrate—"Happy Birthday" and "We Wish You a Merry Christmas," anyone? I sing to cheer. I've gone to a handful of professional soccer games, because I love my kids. And, you all—soccer games have some phenomenal sing-along chants! But mostly I sing along to music that moves me. Typically worship music—at church, in the car, in the kitchen, on a run in the woods—music that reminds me who I am in Jesus, that He is ever faithful, that He is amazing and glorious and all I need.

These are the same reasons King David instructs us to sing. To remind our distracted hearts who God is and that He's on our side. David specifically tells us to sing because God gives us salvation, performs marvelous deeds, created the heavens, and is glorious, worthy, strong, holy, faithful, and just. Those are some pretty stellar reasons.

Those are some of the same reasons thousands upon thousands of angels are singing in the book of Revelation as they stand around the throne of Jesus. And that's pretty cool.

> Then I looked and heard the voice of many angels, numbering thousands upon thousands, and ten thousand times ten thousand. They encircled the throne and the living creatures and the elders. In a loud voice they were saying:
>
> > "Worthy is the Lamb, who was slain,
> >   to receive power and wealth and wisdom
> >   and strength
> >   and honor and glory and praise!"
> >   (5:11–12)

I get goose bumps imagining that throne room. All those angelic voices praising Jesus. Makes me want to sing along.

But some days I'm too focused on *my* stuff, on making sure my forgetful son remembered his lunch, trying to type in the right code to order the online tickets to my daughter's soccer game, swinging by the store to grab a birthday card for my sister-in-law (and some almond milk while I'm there), wiping down the counters, and did I answer that email? My brain tries to remember all those things. My body tries to execute all those things. And in the midst of trying and doing I forget to take time to pause and simply praise the Lord.

But God created my son and daughter, provided clothing and groceries and another year to celebrate my sis-in-law's life. God gave me stories to tell and every single opportunity I've ever had. It would make *more* sense if I took a moment to thank and praise Him, if I was hardly able to contain myself from singing out loud all day long praises and thanks to God for all the blessings He heaps upon me.

Not feeling joyful? Try singing. Just try.

Just like stepping out onto my porch and letting a cardinal's chorus pierce through my swirling thoughts, singing a refrain from a worship song redirects my mind. The cardinal's song makes me push pause and stills me for a moment. It allows me the chance to not just hear his song but glance around in search of him. And then I spot his scarlet feathers and marvel at how brilliant they are, what a gorgeous contrast the red is against the green leaves of the tree he's perched in. And when I sing about standing strong in God's love or that God's arms are open wide to embrace me or simply to thank Jesus for all that He does, it changes something in me. When I raise hallelujahs up to Him or sing that I'm trusting Jesus to stand beside me, never leave me, and fight my battles, my heart shifts. I stop worrying about what I think I need to do. Instead, I'm reminded that I don't want to do anything without Him, that His grace is sufficient for everything I need to do (2 Corinthians 12:9).

I'm guessing the frogs don't put much thought into their songs. Pretty sure the same holds true for the ducks.

They just burst into song because they can, because they're alive and there is air to breathe and water for them to splash in. If creatures with such tiny brains remember to spontaneously sing, shouldn't we?

It doesn't have to be fancy. We don't need to know all the words. We don't even have to have good singing voices (I can't carry a tune). All we need is one word or phrase. "Thank you, Jesus!" or "Jesus loves me, this I know" are both great starts.

There is something tangible about singing out loud. When we actively take part in the song, the truths penetrate deeper into our hearts than if we simply read, heard, or spoke the lyrics.

Science has been hard at work trying to explain why singing has such a calming yet energizing effect on people. What researchers are beginning to discover is that singing is like an infusion of the perfect tranquilizer, the kind that both soothes your nerves and elevates your spirits.[13]

Well, that sounds wonderful: calmer nerves and an elevated mood. No wonder the psalmist instructs us to sing day after day. And that scientific proof is just about singing in general. When we sing to the Lord and recall His truths, His power, His might, His love, we're changed from the inside out.

Whether you have the voice of an angel or you sound more like a frog or a duck, join in with all of creation. You can start right here. Right now. And find some of the peace and joy you're craving.

Sing to the Lord a new song.
Sing to the Lord all the earth.

RESTORE

When was the last time you sang out loud? If it's been awhile, what's holding you back?

Download three new-to-you spiritual songs today onto your device. These could be old hymns or new worship tunes. Try googling the lyrics and singing out loud to at least one of the songs. And then sing along to an old favorite too.

How did the singing make you feel?

23

GRUMBLY OR GRATEFUL

Psalm 104

Praise the LORD, my soul.

LORD my God, you are very great;
*   you are clothed with splendor and majesty.*

The LORD wraps himself in light as with a
*   garment;*
*   he stretches out the heavens like a tent*
*   and lays the beams of his upper chambers*
*   on their waters.*
He makes the clouds his chariot
*   and rides on the wings of the wind.*
He makes winds his messengers,
*   flames of fire his servants.*

He set the earth on its foundations;
*   it can never be moved.*
You covered it with the watery depths as with
*   a garment;*
*   the waters stood above the mountains.*
But at your rebuke the waters fled,
*   at the sound of your thunder they took to*
*   flight;*
they flowed over the mountains,
*   they went down into the valleys,*
*   to the place you assigned for them.*

You set a boundary they cannot cross;
  never again will they cover the earth.

He makes springs pour water into the
    ravines;
  it flows between the mountains.
They give water to all the beasts of the field;
  the wild donkeys quench their thirst.
The birds of the sky nest by the waters;
  they sing among the branches.
He waters the mountains from his upper
    chambers;
  the land is satisfied by the fruit of his
    work.
He makes grass grow for the cattle,
  and plants for people to cultivate—
  bringing forth food from the earth:
wine that gladdens human hearts,
  oil to make their faces shine,
  and bread that sustains their hearts.
The trees of the LORD *are well watered,*
  the cedars of Lebanon that he planted.
There the birds make their nests;
  the stork has its home in the junipers.
The high mountains belong to the wild goats;
  the crags are a refuge for the hyrax.

He made the moon to mark the seasons,
  and the sun knows when to go down.
You bring darkness, it becomes night,
  and all the beasts of the forest prowl.
The lions roar for their prey
  and seek their food from God.
The sun rises, and they steal away;
  they return and lie down in their dens.
Then people go out to their work,
  to their labor until evening.

How many are your works, LORD*!*
  In wisdom you made them all;

187

the earth is full of your creatures.
There is the sea, vast and spacious,
    teeming with creatures beyond number—
    living things both large and small.
There the ships go to and fro,
    and Leviathan, which you formed to frolic
        there.

All creatures look to you
    to give them their food at the proper time.
When you give it to them,
    they gather it up;
when you open your hand,
    they are satisfied with good things.
When you hide your face,
    they are terrified;
when you take away their breath,
    they die and return to the dust.
When you send your Spirit,
    they are created,
    and you renew the face of the ground.

May the glory of the LORD *endure forever;*
    may the LORD *rejoice in his works—*
he who looks at the earth, and it trembles,
    who touches the mountains, and they
        smoke.

I will sing to the LORD *all my life;*
    I will sing praise to my God as long as I
        live.
May my meditation be pleasing to him,
    as I rejoice in the LORD.
But may sinners vanish from the earth
    and the wicked be no more.

Praise the LORD, *my soul.*

Praise the LORD.

When four out of six Smiths got COVID-19, including me, nobody wanted my germy self touching their food or roaming about the kitchen. We sick Smiths were quarantined to our rooms to protect my college-aged daughter and eighth-grade son who miraculously stayed healthy from the virus. And so another morning on the Smith Fam group text began:

> **Maddie:** Are people awake? Can I get anyone food?
> **Max:** I'm up. That would be great.
> **Maddie:** Okay! We have cookies and cream Pop-Tarts that I might have snuck onto the ClickList ☺ Granola? toast?
> **Max:** Pop-Tarts sound fantastic
> **Brett:** Mom and Dad want granola please
> **Maddie:** Any fruit?

Since the day I moved into my first apartment in college, my food has been primarily sourced by me. I do the majority of the grocery shopping, meal planning, and food prep for our family of six. Sometimes the kiddos get creative and cook one of their specialties for us. We get carryout and order pizza on the regular too. But having someone else ask me in the morning what I wanted for breakfast? This was new and just plain weird. Because this was not how I liked to do things. Making oatmeal or even toasting a frozen waffle and pouring some juice for my kids before they head off to school makes me feel good inside—like I got them off to a good start. When one of my kids asks, "What's for dinner?" and I reply, "Homemade mac and cheese," I immediately look to their face to see their expression, knowing I'll be rewarded by a grin, possibly a fist pump, and a response like "Score!"

And so when the two kids took over as chefs and care-takers, becoming fully reliant on them for food and drink caused me to feel all the emotions.

Guilty that it all fell on them to feed the four of us locked behind our bedroom doors.

Frustrated that I couldn't do the things I usually do to help.

And so incredibly grateful that these kids of ours were willing to serve and care for us so intentionally and faithfully.

Even though I'm usually the first person downstairs in the mornings doling out vitamins, writing notes for lunch boxes, and firing up the Nespresso, I didn't go downstairs for fourteen days. That's forty-two consecutive meals served to me. Rich, frothy mochas in the morning hand-crafted by my fellow mocha-loving daughter. PB and Js slathered with sweet strawberry jam and a clementine packed with vitamin C for lunch. Not to mention the dinners our kids cooked for us—ranging from healthy salads to comforting homemade tomato soup. We were also spoiled by friends who delivered bagel sandwiches, freshly baked brownies, and Graeter's ice cream to our doorstep.

And in the process of receiving all this food instead of giving it, God did this beautiful thing in my heart. He made me aware. And grateful. Typically when I want more water, I just go to the kitchen and refill my stain-less-steel water bottle, completely taking it for granted. Now throughout the day Maddie knocked on our door, signaling she'd set bottled waters in the hallway.

Wow! I was thirsty—and now I have water. This feels so good on my throat. Thank you.

Later Maguire would knock and call out, "Your lunch is here."

I was feeling hungry, and here's food. This is fantas-tic. Food I didn't shop for, plan out, or prepare. Food lovingly fixed by my sweet kiddos who didn't just respond to my needs but anticipated them.

I felt flooded by God's blessings. That He kept my youngest and oldest healthy and safe from all the COVID-19 yuck. That they were able to care for us. That God provided us with friends whose generous deliveries always seemed to come at just the moment the kids might need a break from serving (although they never once complained). That our pantry and fridge were full. That my oldest could drive and order groceries online and was willing to pick up our orders. So much provision.

That's who our God is. A provider.

Psalm 104 praises God for His provision and reminds us of all the multifaceted ways God provides.

> He makes springs pour water into the ravines;
>   it flows between the mountains.
> They give water to all the beasts of the field;
>   the wild donkeys quench their thirst.
> The birds of the sky nest by the waters;
>   they sing among the branches.
> He waters the mountains from his upper
>   chambers;
>   the land is satisfied by the fruit of his
>   work.
> He makes grass grow for the cattle,
>   and plants for people to cultivate—
> bringing forth food from the earth:
> wine that gladdens human hearts,
>   oil to make their faces shine,
>   and bread that sustains their hearts.
>   (vv. 10–15)

God does all of that. In just a handful of verses the psalmist shows us how God provides for beasts, donkeys, birds, mountains, land, cattle, and us!

I have been ridiculously blessed my entire life. I've never wondered where my next meal would come from. Sure, there was the year my roommate and I ate pasta every night that her parents mailed us for free from the pasta company they worked for. And there were days in college when either refrigerated canned biscuits or Betty Crocker frosting—yes, straight up frosting from a tub—was my dinner. Not my proudest moments. No judging, please. But there has always been food.

I have friends who have not been so fortunate. Who have eaten from garbage cans, relied on hot lunch programs, and benefited from soup kitchens and churches that provide meals. The stories they share of their need and how they were provided for are both heartbreaking and beautiful in the same breath.

Our God is a provider.

In Exodus 16, millions of Israelites, who had been enslaved by Pharaoh in Egypt, had been freed by God and were now crossing the wilderness to the promised land. They were halfway through their second month of this journey and feared they would starve to death.

> Then the LORD said to Moses, "I will rain down bread from heaven for you." (v. 4)

Because that's normal, right? Raining bread. God is creative and lavish in His provision, and He didn't stop there.

> The LORD said to Moses, "I have heard the grumbling of the Israelites. Tell them, 'At twilight you will eat meat, and in the morning you will be filled with bread. Then you will know that I am the LORD your God.'"
> That evening quail came and covered the camp, and in the morning there was a layer of dew around the camp. When the dew was gone, thin flakes like frost on the ground appeared on the desert floor. When the Israelites

saw it, they said to each other, "What is it?" For they did not know what it was.

Moses said to them, "It is the bread the LORD has given you to eat." (vv. 11–15)

God provided food in the desert.
To millions of people.
For forty years.
Why?
So they would know that He was their Lord and God. That He was their provider. That should make it pretty obvious, right? They depended on God day and night for survival, and day and night He gave them exactly what they needed. Clearly the Israelites could see He was a God who loved and cared for them.

You would think so, but two years later the Israelites who were still wandering around the wilderness were complaining about the bread (called manna) that God daily provided on the ground for them.

We remember the fish we used to eat for free in Egypt. And we had all the cucumbers, melons, leeks, onions, and garlic we wanted. But now our appetites are gone. All we ever see is this manna!" (Numbers 11:5–6 NLT)

Oh, sorry, you're in the middle of the desert and every single day God provides you manna that tastes like sweet pastries prepared with olive oil, and you wish you had some fish and garlic?

Those Israelites sound so whiny.

Until I consider myself.

"Um, I think they gave me the wrong kind of cheese on my sandwich."

Or, "Did they forget the peppermint in my peppermint mocha?"

Or, "Doesn't the crust look a little burnt?"

Ugh!

When God provides us so much, why do we grumble?

If someone makes or gives you a meal, do you complain that it's not to your exact liking? Or are you grateful?

If you have a full agenda on your work calendar, are you grumbling that you don't have time to sit and read a book by yourself or grab lunch with pals? Or are you thankful that God has given you a job that pays your bills?

If there is a heap o' laundry in the hamper, are you whining about how much there is? Or praising God for your family whose clothes need to be washed, a washing machine in which to wash them, hands capable of folding?

I'm not pointing fingers here. I'm asking these questions to myself too. And I'm convicted. God provides so abundantly. So, why? Why do I complain? I'd rather be grateful than grumbly. I want to be like the psalmist who began and ended Psalm 104 rich in descriptions of God's provision with thanks and praise.

> Praise the LORD, my soul.

> LORD my God, you are very great;
>   you are clothed with splendor and majesty.
>   (v. 1)

> I will sing to the LORD all my life;
>   I will sing praise to my God as long as I
>   live.
> May my meditation be pleasing to him,
>   as I rejoice in the LORD. (vv. 33–34)

Only weeks after coming out of quarantine, I found it strange how quickly I took for granted that if I was hungry in the middle of the day I could grab an apple from the top of the fridge (actually selecting the specific apple I wanted) or a handful of semisweet chocolate chips from the little plastic tub in the cupboard where we keep our baking ingredients.

I think of Paul's instructions to the church in Thessalonica: "Rejoice always, pray continually, give thanks in all circumstances; for this is God's will for you in Christ Jesus" (1 Thessalonians 5:16–18).

And I want to do this. I want to be like Paul and the psalmist, constantly rejoicing, praying, and giving thanks (the opposite of grumbling) because God is constantly providing for me in ways that blow me away, in ways I can't even see, and in ways I take for granted.

We can rejoice in the multitude of provisions God has gifted us. It can be as easy as thanking Him for a sweet, juicy orange or a family member who handed it to us. We can start right now. And once we get started, it's mind-blowing how our gratitude grows.

Ann Voskamp, the author of *One Thousand Gifts*, says, "Gratitude is at the center of a life of faith. It sounds too simple to be true, but isn't that the sign of all deep truth: so simple we're tempted to dismiss it, and so hard, it is exactly what God uses to change our lives."[14]

I love that God can use something as simple as us giving thanks to change hard situations, to aid in our struggles, to rescue us from pain, to replace hardships with joy. I want this. And so I'm making it my aim to let all that I am praise the Lord! Will you join me?

--- RESTORE ---

Have you grumbled about anything lately? Take a moment to ask God to forgive you and show you how to best address your frustration.

Now, what are you thankful for today? What has God provided for you? Don't just list one

thing—try listing ten, and if you're on a roll, keep
going.

Take a moment to thank God for each of those
things. Out loud. It's easy. But also powerful.
Saying these things out loud helps us hold onto
the blessings at hand and remind ourselves what
a provider our God is. It can be as simple as,
"Thank you, God, for the text from my friend
that made me smile. Thank you, God, that my
headache is gone. Thank you, God, that I have a
car with gas in the tank and can go where I need
to go today." Now you try . . .

24

SOCCER BALLS AND SPACIOUS PLACES

Psalm 118

Give thanks to the LORD, for he is good;
  his love endures forever.

Let Israel say:
  "His love endures forever."
Let the house of Aaron say:
  "His love endures forever."
Let those who fear the LORD say:
  "His love endures forever."

When hard pressed, I cried to the LORD;
  he brought me into a spacious place.
The LORD is with me; I will not be afraid.
  What can mere mortals do to me?
The LORD is with me; he is my helper.
  I look in triumph on my enemies. . . .

The LORD is my strength and my defense;
  he has become my salvation.

Shouts of joy and victory
  resound in the tents of the righteous:
"The LORD's right hand has done mighty
    things!
  The LORD's right hand is lifted high;
  the LORD's right hand has done mighty
    things!" . . .

LORD, save us!
LORD, grant us success!

Blessed is he who comes in the name of the
LORD.
From the house of the LORD we bless you.
The LORD is God,
and he has made his light shine on us.
With boughs in hand, join in the festal
procession
up to the horns of the altar.

You are my God, and I will praise you;
you are my God, and I will exalt you.

Give thanks to the LORD, for he is good;
his love endures forever. (vv. 1–7, 14–16,
25–29)

Whack! A bullet of a soccer ball careened toward my son's head, hitting him at full speed and force. It was his fourth concussion. He'd made the varsity team as a freshman and had been playing ever since. But now this. An unexpected early ending.

Our boy felt abandoned, lost, and mad. It didn't feel fair. He was unable to play the game he'd always played and uninvited by necessity to the daily practices and games of his soccer buddies. He endured countless headaches and days of dizziness.

It broke our hearts knowing our boy wouldn't get the rest of his junior or any of his senior season, a senior night, his locker decorated, the daily interaction with his teammates, the camaraderie of it all. This thing that was so much of our son's high school experience no longer was.

My husband and I prayed. For our son's injured head.

For his disappointment, anger, fear, and pain. We asked God for healing. That God would remind him he was loved. We continued praying through that fall, winter, spring, summer, and the following fall. We knew God was with us. We knew He loved us, and He blessed us in all kinds of ways. But for over a year our son felt sidelined both physically and socially. We kept praying.

We never once asked God for indoor track.

I didn't even know it was a thing.

But that's how God answered our prayers.

The night before forms signed by parents for winter sports were due, our son came into our room as I was brushing my teeth and asked if I would give him permission to run. I spit out the minty foam and gladly clicked the appropriate boxes on the online form he'd pulled up on his school-issued iPad, grateful there was a way he could be active and engage with classmates outside of the classroom.

Our boy is fast. And the sport suited him. His relay team made it to the state finals. But even better? The team!

These kids he met in the middle of his senior year became some of his favorite people from high school. They were the nicest kids. They worked hard, pushing themselves to beat their own times, but they also genuinely cared for and supported one another. They invited our son into their lives and embraced him for exactly who he was.

God hadn't just given him a new sport but a way to move his eighteen-year-old body (if you've ever been around teenage boys, you know this is critical) and a priceless set of friends. Our son went to senior prom with kids from the track team. The summer after graduation he ran almost daily with this crew of pals. His two freshman roommates in college were guys who ran at his high school. And running? It's become a daily ritual for our boy to exercise while allowing his mind to process all the things bouncing around in a college boy's brain.

Our son never got to play soccer again. But God *did* answer our prayers. God didn't renew soccer or replace what soccer had been. He gave our boy so much more than he'd ever known or felt on the pitch.

In our initial sadness and confusion, we hadn't been sure what to ask for. And that was all right. God doesn't expect us to know the best way to solve all the problems. So He gives us a hand. As Paul tells the Romans, "We do not know what we ought to pray for, but the Spirit himself intercedes for us through wordless groans" (8:26).

This is how God works.

Have you seen it in action? You asked God for something, and He answered, but in a grander way than you expected. In a way that also blessed others or answered multiple prayers—even ones you didn't know you had. We ask for a grouper, and sometimes God gives us fishing lessons, a net, a rod, a boat, and a stocked bait box. Our limited brains didn't know to ask for all that! God gives more abundantly and incredibly. He's so cool like that.

This isn't just my opinion. Paul tells the church in Ephesus, "Now to [Jesus] who is able to do immeasurably more than all we ask or imagine, according to his power that is at work within us . . ." (Ephesians 3:20). Jesus works outside the realm of our wildest dreams when it comes to answering prayers.

Maybe you're like we were, over a year into our prayers for our boy. Maybe you're still waiting. Psalm 118 invites us in our pain and fear to cry out to God, "LORD, save us!" (v. 25). Even when we feel our prayer hasn't been answered, God is still able to do more than we can ask or imagine. It might seem bleak right now, but God is at work. He might be doing something that will blow us away next week, next year, or on the other side of heaven. God's love endures forever.

The psalmist emphasizes this truth in verse 1, "Give thanks to the LORD, for he is good; his love endures forever." I love that the writer continues:

> Let Israel say:
> "His love endures forever."
> Let the house of Aaron say:
> "His love endures forever."
> Let those who fear the LORD say:
> "His love endures forever." (vv. 2–4)

The psalmist doesn't want to stop at thanking God for His goodness and love, but wants everyone else to join in. Perhaps, like me, the psalmist also saw God answer not just a specific prayer but, in so doing, multiple prayers. I could write,

> Give thanks to God for He is so good;
> His love endures forever.

> Let my husband, my son, and me all
> proclaim:
> "His love endures forever."
> Let my son's state relay team proclaim,
> "His love endures forever."
> Let his roommates proclaim,
> "His love endures forever."

The psalmist goes on to say:

> When hard pressed, I cried to the LORD;
> he brought me into a spacious place.
> The LORD is with me; I will not be afraid.
> What can mere mortals do to me? (vv. 5–6)

Like the psalmist, my husband and I were hard-pressed and called out to God. God placed our boy in a spacious place. A place way bigger than soccer. Track wasn't just a sport but more meaningful friendships, roommates, and a long-term physical and mental health tool. The Lord was with our boy. Just like God is with me. And God is with you. He's working behind the scenes even when we don't see it—putting this in place, sliding that over there. We really have nothing to fear.

If we hadn't cried out to God, would our son have joined indoor track? Perhaps.

A friend might have nudged him to join the team. He might have gotten sick of not moving, heard an announcement at school, and just given it a try. I'll never know.

But if I hadn't cried out, I would never have been able to see the valiant things God's right hand did (v. 16). Sure, I would have seen how happy my boy was and how good indoor track was for him, but I might not have directly attributed these to God answering prayers. To God's faithfulness. To the power of prayer. And if I hadn't witnessed God so beautifully answering my prayers, then I wouldn't understand how He is my strength and my song (v. 14 NLT). That God almighty heard me. That He moved in phenomenal ways.

I want to see those things. I want to see God in action, so I can remember.

Because I'll have more prayer requests.

Daily.

Sometimes I'll travel a long, hard road before I see any of them being answered.

And I want to hold onto the truth that God hears our prayers. That He listens to us when we cry out to Him. That He so graciously responds. That we can count on God to defend us and the people we love.

Today I'm praying for a friend's surgery to successfully heal her ailment, for another friend who just moved to find community in her new home, for my kids to not be so stressed this last week of their semester despite their heavy schoolwork loads, for a woman whose marriage is in shambles. All these things are out of my control. But all things are within God's wheelhouse. And because I've seen Him work so extravagantly in the past, because I've seen God respond to my cries, I can pray with the psalmist, "You are my God, and I will praise you; you are my God, and I will exalt you" (v. 28).

When I ask Jesus for the things I've listed and so many more, I can be confident:

1. God is good.
2. God's love endures forever.
3. Therefore He will hear and respond to my prayers.

Maybe not how I envisioned.

In fact, probably not at all how I envisioned, but in rich, gorgeous, powerful ways. Since God is fully good, He wants good. He does good. He's incapable of doing bad. Instead, God takes bad things and uses them for good (Romans 8:28). And since His love never expires (it endures forever), I don't have to wonder if He's listening today or if I've met my quota on prayer requests. God is always listening.

Talking to Jesus, crying out to Him, does not guarantee that hard things won't come our way. They will. We live in a broken world where hate, lust, greed, disease, and runaway soccer balls run rampant. But God wants us to tell Him about our woes and worries. When we cry out to the Lord, He listens. He responds. Not necessarily how we asked. But always in wide-spanning, thoughtful, impactful ways.

There might be times when it feels like your prayers have gone unanswered. What then? We'd prefer for God to move on our timelines, but He works on an almighty clock and calendar, which look way different than ours.

I prayed for healing for my father-in-law, and he died.

In my father-in-law's final breaths, he whispered from his hospital bed to my husband that he was ready to be with God. Up until then Rick didn't believe in God. And Rick certainly wouldn't have looked forward to being with someone he didn't believe in. Somewhere in the middle of my father-in-law's pain, as he slipped in and out of consciousness, God came to him and healed something so much more important than his body: his soul. My prayer *was* answered. And if Rick had never told anyone this miracle or if he had spoken it to a nurse or one of his buddies instead of my husband, I might not have ever known. But God still did it. Whether I knew about it or not. Something grander than what I'd prayed for. It's like that old question: If a tree falls in a forest and no one is there, would it still make a sound?

Of course it would.

Many of our prayers are answered in empty forests.

I love verse 5 of this psalm so much: "He brought me into a spacious place."

It's a great way to describe the impact of a winter sport that didn't just give my son's athletic body something to do but gave him new purpose and community that went beyond the walls and days of high school and on to college.

Spacious is not just a body healing but a soul healing, one that means our family will get to dance with my father-in-law in heaven one day.

Spacious. That's who our God is. Cry out to Him.

— RESTORE —

What's on your heart today? What's worrying you, bothering you, keeping you up at night? Have you cried out to God about it? Take time to do so now (either for the first time or again).

Can you recall a time when God answered a prayer completely differently than you'd hoped or considered, but He definitely answered? Write about it here. End your journaling with these words: "Give thanks to the Lord. His love endures forever."

25

GRAND PLANS AND DETAILS

Psalm 119

Blessed are those whose ways are blameless,
who walk according to the law of the
    LORD.
Blessed are those who keep his statutes
    and seek him with all their heart—
they do no wrong
    but follow his ways.
You have laid down precepts
    that are to be fully obeyed.
Oh, that my ways were steadfast
    in obeying your decrees!
Then I would not be put to shame
    when I consider all your commands.
I will praise you with an upright heart
    as I learn your righteous laws.
I will obey your decrees;
    do not utterly forsake me.

How can a young person stay on the path of
        purity?
    By living according to your word.
I seek you with all my heart;
    do not let me stray from your commands.
I have hidden your word in my heart

that I might not sin against you.
Praise be to you, LORD;
   teach me your decrees.
With my lips I recount
   all the laws that come from your mouth.
I rejoice in following your statutes
   as one rejoices in great riches.
I meditate on your precepts
   and consider your ways.
I delight in your decrees;
   I will not neglect your word. . . .

I reach out for your commands, which I love,
   that I may meditate on your decrees.

Remember your word to your servant,
   for you have given me hope.
My comfort in my suffering is this:
   Your promise preserves my life.
The arrogant mock me unmercifully,
   but I do not turn from your law.
I remember, LORD, your ancient laws,
   and I find comfort in them.
Indignation grips me because of the wicked,
   who have forsaken your law.
Your decrees are the theme of my song
   wherever I lodge.
In the night, LORD, I remember your name,
   that I may keep your law.
This has been my practice:
   I obey your precepts. . . .

My soul faints with longing for your
      salvation,
   but I have put my hope in your word. . . .

How sweet are your words to my taste,
   sweeter than honey to my mouth!
I gain understanding from your precepts;
   therefore I hate every wrong path.

Your word is a lamp for my feet,
   a light on my path.
I have taken an oath and confirmed it,
    that I will follow your righteous laws.
I have suffered much;
     preserve my life, LORD, according to your
       word.
Accept, LORD, the willing praise of my mouth,
   and teach me your laws.
Though I constantly take my life in my hands,
   I will not forget your law.
The wicked have set a snare for me,
    but I have not strayed from your precepts.
Your statutes are my heritage forever;
   they are the joy of my heart.
My heart is set on keeping your decrees
   to the very end.

I hate double-minded people,
   but I love your law.
You are my refuge and my shield;
   I have put my hope in your word.
Away from me, you evildoers,
   that I may keep the commands of my God!
Sustain me, my God, according to your
      promise, and I will live;
   do not let my hopes be dashed.
Uphold me, and I will be delivered;
   I will always have regard for your decrees.
You reject all who stray from your decrees,
   for their delusions come to nothing.
All the wicked of the earth you discard like
     dross;
   therefore I love your statutes.
My flesh trembles in fear of you;
   I stand in awe of your laws.

I have done what is righteous and just;
   do not leave me to my oppressors.

Ensure your servant's well-being;
  do not let the arrogant oppress me.
My eyes fail, looking for your salvation,
  looking for your righteous promise.
Deal with your servant according to your
      love
and teach me your decrees.
I am your servant; give me discernment
  that I may understand your statutes.
It is time for you to act, LORD;
  your law is being broken.
Because I love your commands
  more than gold, more than pure gold.
      (vv. 1–16, 48–56, 81, 103–27)

I booked the hotel and the flights." My husband's smile lights up his face.

Brett loves planning travel, especially if it's a romantic getaway. Our annual escapes have been as simple as staying one night in a hotel a mile from my mom's condo and as extravagant as a trip to the coast of Italy. We do this because we recognize marriage as a gift from God. One that needs to be nurtured, fed, and watered. These trips do that for us. To clarify, Brett loves planning the big-picture items of travel.

Me? I'm in charge of the details. Brett does his part—usually a year in advance, talking about when and where we should go for our next excursion, getting me to commit to something long before it would have been on my radar. He thoroughly enjoys browsing through Vrbo and trying multiple flight options, figuring out that if we left on Wednesday our flights could be 128 dollars cheaper. Months prior to our trip he's finished with his part. Which is awesome. I'm beyond grateful he tends to the large pieces of our travel plans. But I'm just getting started.

I email our kids' teachers and coaches and arrange for rides. I have countless chats about the details with my mom, who is the absolute loveliest human and graciously agrees to care for our children while we're gone. I type out a day-by-day agenda for her, complete with where everyone needs to be and when, food allergies, and phone numbers of friends in case Mom needs help with anything. If a form can be filled out ahead of time, I sign it. I stock the fridge and pantry, do the laundry, put Brett's and my vitamins in baggies to take with us, make sure we have sunscreen, passports, travel snacks, and any other necessary items packed. I'm taking care of my end of the planning up to the moment we leave our house.

And it works.

Brett's big-picture planning and my detail organizing allow us to enjoy restful time away together in lovely places at lower prices without having to worry whether Maguire has a black T-shirt for his upcoming play or who will cheer Mallory on at her soccer game. Both the larger pieces and the specifics are important for our safety, peace, and enjoyment. Brett and I need each other to pull a trip together and make it work.

The fine print and the overview are also important in our life journeys.

Thankfully, God excels at both. God created our galaxy, which has an estimated 100–400 billion (yup, with a *b*) stars.[15] And that's just one galaxy out of an estimated 2,000 billion galaxies in the observable universe.[16] God is the master of the infinite. And God is also the expert at details, such as the 37.2 trillion tiny cells in one human body.[17]

And because God is phenomenal at both grandiose and minute things, He put both in Scripture, for us to have everything we need for our trips through life—the big picture and the details.

Psalm 119 is the longest of the psalms with a whopping

176 verses. It spans five pages in my Bible and was written as an intricate piece of poetry with one stanza for each letter of the Hebrew alphabet.

C. S. Lewis calls Psalm 119 "a thing done like embroidery, stitch by stitch, through long, quiet hours, for love of the subject and for the delight in leisurely, disciplined craftsmanship."[18]

But Psalm 119 is more than a piece of poetry. It's a love letter, not about a person but about God's words to His people. The psalmist writes all those verses about how wonderful God's instruction to us is.

> With my lips I recount
>   all the laws that come from your mouth.
> I rejoice in following your statutes
>   as one rejoices in great riches.
> I meditate on your precepts
>   and consider your ways.
> I delight in your decrees;
>   I will not neglect your word. (vv. 13–16)

Why does the psalmist love God's law so much? Because God's words have guided the psalmist through both the big events in their life and the everyday details, through afflictions, lies, wicked people, and sorrow. God's words have held up the psalmist, given them hope, and directed their ways. The Torah (what existed of the Bible at that time) guided the writer of Psalm 119. The Bible can do the same for us if we too savor it like sweet honey and treasure it like pure gold:

> How sweet are your words to my taste,
>   sweeter than honey to my mouth! (v. 103)

> Because I love your commands
>   more than gold, more than pure gold.
>   (v. 127)

God knew we would need big ideas to anchor ourselves with, so He puts lots of these in the Bible. He also put tiny details in the Bible because He knew we'd need them for deeper understanding and personal connection. We'll get to those details in just a minute. For now, let's talk about the big ideas. One I play on repeat is that Christ offers us peace: "Peace I leave with you; my peace I give you. I do not give to you as the world gives. Do not let your hearts be troubled and do not be afraid" (John 14:27).

When my husband heads into his cardiology appointment, or I'm frazzled after being on hold with the insurance company for twenty-three minutes, or I'm stuck behind a train and late to pick up one of my kids from their field trip, or I get a nasty email that tangles up my insides, I can remember to inhale Christ's peace, because Jesus promises over and over again in the pages of the Bible that He'll provide it for me, for us.

Another one of the big ideas repeated throughout Scripture that I really need is forgiveness. I don't know about you, but mistakes from my past haunt me. I'll be driving along and it's like someone changes the slide on a PowerPoint from a picture of the road in front of me to the time I did that shameful thing or said those words or acted in that way. When this happens, I need to shake my head and get those ugly thoughts out of there. Like the author of Psalm 119, I need to beg God to "open my eyes that I may see wonderful things in your law" (v. 18).

When I do, when I reach out to Jesus, He reminds me of the truth from Ephesians 1:7: "In him we have redemption through his blood, the forgiveness of sins, in accordance with the riches of God's grace." And I can cling to the fact that Jesus has forgiven me. For everything. That His grace has been lavished on me (and you too). I can talk to Jesus about my regrets, and He reassures me that His love conquered all those past sins as well as any I'll make tomorrow and the day after that. Then my mental slideshow returns to the current time and place of a regularly scheduled after-school pickup.

You might have your own favorite big ideas from Scripture that infiltrate your days, that you use as your screen saver or have scrawled across your calendar, stuck to your mirror, or marked up in your Bible. Or you might be new to the Bible, trying to figure out what it actually means. Either way, opening the pages of God's Word exposes us to these fundamental truths, etches them on our souls, so when we need them we can avoid the smoke and mirrors, distractions, and lies that come at us from this world and instead keep our thoughts centered on reality, on truth.

But God also wants us to know the specifics. Details in the Bible can take the historic accounts and make them deeply personal. There's this passage in Mark 5 and Luke 8 where Jesus calls a woman "daughter." Which doesn't sound like a huge deal if you skim past it or if you're looking at the big picture. There is an overarching theme to this passage—that Jesus is a healer. He heals this woman of a bleeding disorder she's had for twelve years, like He heals so many others. And that's an awesome big idea. Jesus heals! Hallelujah!

But as I read about this outcast of a woman who works her way through the crowd to get close enough to Jesus to touch His cloak and is immediately healed, my ears perk up when Jesus looks at her and says, "Daughter, your faith has healed you" (Mark 5:34). That little detail. That Jesus calls this unclean, unwanted woman "daughter." That Jesus calls her something you only say to someone you cherish. It wrecks me. And changes me. That detail reminds me when I feel like I don't belong or that I won't measure up that Jesus also calls me "daughter." He looks us in the eye, no matter how badly we're bleeding—bleeding regret, bleeding anger, bleeding sorrow, bleeding shame, bleeding fear—and says, "Daughter/ Son, I see you in this. I love you. I can heal you too."

All because the authors of Mark and Luke when they sat down to share this story were prompted by God to share this detail, this single word.

The Word of God is packed with thousands of details—ones that might speak to you today or next week or fifteen years from now—that God has nestled within its stories, pages, and accounts to touch you and me personally.

The more often I read God's words, the easier it is to remember them, the more natural it feels to apply them, the more often they spring to mind. It's cool to see how true that was for this psalmist centuries ago. That God's word was exciting and healing and invigorating and comforting then, just like it is now.

> Your word is a lamp for my feet,
>   a light on my path. (v. 105)

> I have put my hope in your word. (v. 81)

> You have given me hope.
> My comfort in my suffering is this:
>   Your promise preserves my life. (vv. 49–50)

Yes, Lord!

As I think about all the times the Bible has encouraged or strengthened me, given me hope or direction, I declare with the psalmist, "I reach out for your commands, which I love, that I may meditate on your decrees" (v. 48).

Our journeys through life are definitely complicated. But God gives us one book that provides us with our itinerary, our instruction manual, a boarding pass (John 3:16), and a place to stay (14:2). The Bible also provides us with a compass (14:6), a flashlight (8:12), and all the incidentals we'll need along the way. God has made sure that He's packed our bags with exactly what we need to make decisions big and small, to deal with both ginormous challenges and accomplishments and tiny nuisances and triumphs.

Yes, Lord, "the unfolding of your words gives light" (v. 130). The light that guides our footsteps no matter where we're headed.

——————————— RESTORE ———————————

Read Psalm 119 this week. Jot down both one big idea that caught your eye and one detail that resonated with you.

26

NIGHT WATCHMAN

Psalm 121

I lift up my eyes to the mountains—
  where does my help come from?
My help comes from the Lord,
  the Maker of heaven and earth.

He will not let your foot slip—
  he who watches over you will not slumber;
indeed, he who watches over Israel
  will neither slumber nor sleep.

The Lord *watches over you—*
  the Lord *is your shade at your right hand;*
the sun will not harm you by day,
  nor the moon by night.

The Lord *will keep you from all harm—*
  he will watch over your life;
the Lord *will watch over your coming and*
        going
  both now and forevermore.

Like most American kids I was

1. afraid of the dark; and
2. required to read *A Wrinkle in Time.*

It turns out these two seemingly unrelated plot points connected around sixth grade.

At that time I slept with my closet door cracked open and the light inside switched on, allowing a comforting golden glow to spill into my room at night. I also was thrilled to discover that the author of *A Wrinkle in Time* (which I loved) had more books for me to read. I dove headfirst into Madeleine L'Engle's Austin Family Chronicles series. After finishing the first title, I picked up the second, *The Moon by Night*, about a fourteen-year-old girl on a summer trip with her family and all the early teenage drama. I was surprised when I got to page 240, where Vicky Austin recited Psalm 121.

Vicky wasn't in church or at youth group or alone in her room reading her Bible. She was in danger and speaking this psalm out loud in front of an unbelieving peer. The words didn't do magic, convert her friend, resolve all the problems, or completely calm her. But they did something. There was a shift. Reciting the psalm changed Vicky's outlook and her situation. And in the midst of reading that night in my brass bed with the white eyelet bedspread, surrounded by my favorite stuffed animals, I looked up Psalm 121 in my Bible. And you know what? It was exactly how it read in my novel. The powerful words penetrated.

> The LORD watches over you—
>   the LORD is your shade at your right hand;
> the sun will not harm you by day,
>   nor the moon by night. (vv. 5–6)

These words placed the God from church, the God I read about in my Bible, right next to me. Watching over me. All the time. I hadn't realized that before—that He was accessible, near. I'd viewed church and prayers as one distinct part of my life, and everything else as another.

But in reality—they were all entwined. God was with me in the daytime while I turned the pages of paperbacks, walked to and from school, and pirouetted at the old church with glossy wood floors converted into a dance studio where I took ballet lessons. He was with me at night in my room with the sky-blue walls when I heard creepy noises and tried to find comfort in the light escaping the crack in my closet door. In all those times God was watching over me.

That same night I woke up around two in the morning, spooked. Which was a regular thing for me. Startling nightmares. But the words of the psalm came to mind:

"Nor the moon by night."

I repeated it over and over in my head. The lines before it were something about God staying awake all night, keeping an eye out for me even while I snoozed. I loved that imagery but couldn't recall the words. I held onto the mental picture and fell back asleep.

> He will not let your foot slip—
>   he who watches over you will not slumber;
> indeed, he who watches over Israel
>   will neither slumber nor sleep. (vv. 3–4)

In the morning I was convinced of God's presence watching over me while I slept, and after years of being terrified of the dark, I exhaled. I underlined the words in my Bible, thinking it was so cool that Vicky Austin, who was depicted on the book's cover wearing jeans and sitting next to a cute boy, must also have these words in her Bible marked. (Yes, I realize she's a fictional character, but the characters in books were so real to me growing up. Okay, sometimes still.)

Psalm 121 revealed something totally new to me about God. God was my constant protector.

From then on when I had a nightmare or heard creaks

in the night, I returned to this psalm over and over. When babysitting, once the kids I was watching were in bed and I was alone in a strange house, these words were a comfort—the sun shall not smite me by day nor the moon by night. I don't know if I fully believed them yet, but I tried willing them to be true.

I sleep remarkably well these days, but there are nights when my big kids are out late and I wake and wonder, Are they home yet? Did they forget to come in and tell me good night? Are they safe driving in the dark? In the rain? Or when my husband travels and although we texted at midday I don't know if he made it safely back to his hotel. Is he safe in that city? Or I have a doctor's appointment the next day. Not a checkup but a follow-up. Which is very different. What will the tests find?

And now from muscle memory these words come in blips. I've read them and prayed them enough times that it takes almost nothing to bring them to mind; they just appear. My help comes from the Lord. He will not let my foot slip. He who watches over me, who watches over Israel, will not slumber or sleep. The sun shall not smite me by day nor the moon by night. And these words proclaiming God's faithfulness, that He is my protector, drown out the worry. I don't necessarily fall asleep immediately, but the thought spirals of "what if?" are shut down, because I'm thinking of a moon glowing warmly and a Night Watchman who promises to stay awake and guard me.

We see God in many ways because He is multifaceted. He is Creator, Savior, Healer, King, Judge, Best Friend, Miracle Worker, Redeemer, Bridegroom, Rescuer, Prince of Peace. But He is also Protector. And we can't lose sight of that.

God has always been our protector. And always will be.

In 2 Kings 6:15–17 the king of Aram was furious with the prophet Elisha for thwarting his plans to attack the

Israelites. Under the cover of night the king sent horses and chariots to surround Elisha and his people, hoping to destroy them.

> When the servant of [Elisha] got up and went out early the next morning, an army with horses and chariots had surrounded the city. "Oh no, my lord! What shall we do?" the servant asked.
>
> "Don't be afraid," the prophet [Elisha] answered. "Those who are with us are more than those who are with them."
>
> And Elisha prayed, "Open his eyes, LORD, so that he may see." Then the LORD opened the servant's eyes, and he looked and saw the hills full of horses and chariots of fire all around Elisha.

God filled the hills with His angel armies, way out-numbering the enemy and keeping His people safe. Normal, right?

Well, for God it is.

In Daniel 3 King Nebuchadnezzar ordered that three Hebrews living in Babylon, Shadrach, Meshach, and Abednego, be tied up and thrown in a fiery furnace because they refused to bow down to a golden statue of him.

Nebuchadnezzar, who was watching the whole thing, shouted, "Look! I see four men walking around in the fire, unbound and unharmed, and the fourth looks like a son of the gods" (v. 25). Nebuchadnezzar then approached the opening of the blazing furnace and called out:

> "Shadrach, Meshach and Abednego, servants of the Most High God, come out! Come here!"
>
> So Shadrach, Meshach and Abednego came out of the fire, and the satraps, prefects, governors and royal advisers crowded around them. They saw that the fire had not

harmed their bodies, nor was a hair of their heads singed; their robes were not scorched, and there was no smell of fire on them. (vv. 26–27)

Wait, what? Their clothes didn't have burn marks? They didn't even smell like smoke? How did they get untied? And who do you think that fourth man who looked like "a son of the gods" was walking around in there with them?

It was Jesus, our protector.

This isn't just an Old Testament concept. Paul tells the Thessalonians in his second letter to their church, "But the Lord is faithful, and he will strengthen you and protect you from the evil one" (3:3).

What do you need protection from today? Loneliness? Debt? Systemic injustice? Is someone or something causing or threatening harm? Are you being dangerous toward yourself?

Jesus is your protector. He is the God of angel armies. On most days as I pray, I'm thinking of Jesus as my friend that I can tell anything to. Which He is. But it's critical to remember as I confide in Him that He's way more than a good listener. He is actually the one who can do something about all the scary, looming things in my life and in this world. Jesus has pulled people from flames, guarded them from advancing armies, healed them from diseases, calmed storms, and even hurried an entire family plus two of every kind of animal into a giant boat as a safe haven from a forty-day rainstorm and flood (#Noah).

He can and will protect you too. I'm not sure what that will look like. We humans don't always understand God's ways, but I do know He loves you and longs for you to be safe. Will you ask Him for this protection? Will you trust Jesus to do the saving? In the dark of night will you call out His name?

In the midst of fear this isn't always the easiest thing to do. Sometimes during fright we want to run or hide or scream or flail. When our adrenaline is coursing and our fear is rising, we're rarely rational. Which is why memorizing a short psalm can really come in handy.

Psalm 121 is only eight verses long—a quick and easy one to memorize. The words work like a weapon against fear and anxiety. John, the disciple who calls himself the one Jesus loved, reminds us that perfect love casts out fear (1 John 4:18). Jesus, our protector, the one who is perfect love, can cast out our fears. Reminding ourselves of this love—that He won't let our feet slip, that He will keep us from harm, that He will watch over our lives, that He will watch our comings and goings now and always—makes that fear flee.

And then we can exhale. We can welcome the sunlight of a new day, knowing God is at our side protecting us. We can close our eyes at night, knowing in the glow of the moonlight that our Night Watchman has never once fallen asleep or been caught off guard on His shift. And even on days when we're not sure what we're up against, or we're not certain we fully believe the words, we can, like Vicky Austin or my sixth-grade-with-thick-rainbow-colored-plastic-glasses-and-a-mouth-full-of-braces self, proclaim them out loud and let the declaration of these truths shift what's going on, defuse our fear, and remind us and the enemy who is actually in charge. The almighty, all-powerful God who commands the seas and winds, who is on our side, and who is watching over us, protecting us, keeping us safe. Now. And always.

——————— RESTORE ———————

What are you afraid of during the day? At night?

Write out verse 6 over your fears: "The sun will not harm you by day, nor the moon by night." Or try another version like the Passion Translation: "He's protecting you from all danger both day and night."

Commit Psalm 121:6 to memory today. Read or write it over and over again until you can recite it by heart. For an added challenge, work on memorizing the entire psalm this week.

27

TWELFTH OF NEVER

Psalm 136

Give thanks to the LORD, *for he is good.*
  His love endures forever.
Give thanks to the God of gods.
  His love endures forever.
Give thanks to the Lord of lords:
  His love endures forever.

to him who alone does great wonders,
  His love endures forever.
who by his understanding made the heavens,
  His love endures forever.
who spread out the earth upon the waters,
  His love endures forever.
who made the great lights—
  His love endures forever.
the sun to govern the day,
  His love endures forever.
the moon and stars to govern the night;
  His love endures forever.

to him who struck down the firstborn of
          Egypt
  His love endures forever.
and brought Israel out from among them
  His love endures forever.
with a mighty hand and outstretched arm;
  His love endures forever.

to him who divided the Red Sea asunder
His love endures forever.
and brought Israel through the midst of it,
His love endures forever.
but swept Pharaoh and his army into the Red
Sea;
His love endures forever.

to him who led his people through the
wilderness;
His love endures forever.

to him who struck down great kings,
His love endures forever.
and killed mighty kings—
His love endures forever.
Sihon king of the Amorites
His love endures forever.
and Og king of Bashan—
His love endures forever.
and gave their land as an inheritance,
His love endures forever.
an inheritance to his servant Israel.
His love endures forever.

He remembered us in our low estate
His love endures forever.
and freed us from our enemies.
His love endures forever.
He gives food to every creature.
His love endures forever.

Give thanks to the God of heaven.
His love endures forever.

My dad collects records—those black vinyl discs that were invented before cassettes, and before CDs, and way, way before Spotify. He grew up in the fifties and sixties, so songs from those decades are his favorites. One tune that spun on his turntable when I was a little girl made me dream of fairy-tale romance, "The Twelfth of Never." In this song the singer tells his true love how his love will last forever and ever, until flowers lose their fragrance and no longer bloom, until the twelfth of never. Which is a nonsensical phrase, but it's trying to emphasize that they will love this person forever, until a date that won't ever get here!

A love like that was the love I longed for. Most of us do. We long to be loved and cherished and for that love to never expire. But personally, throughout high school and college I questioned if that kind of love was attainable. I had a serious relationship in high school with a great guy, but when we went our separate ways to colleges in different states, we grew in different directions. I had a run of romances in college—ranging from falling for the handsome, broody biker boy I got set up with to kissing the boy with the dazzling green eyes from the party to going out with the guy from my group project in marketing class to dating the fun-loving, smiley guy to getting back together with my high school ex-boyfriend over the summer only to discover that still wasn't going to work. Just writing about it makes me dizzy. And let's just say all of them were far from the twelfth of never.

By the time I was twenty-two, I'd pretty much decided there was no such thing as lasting love. And it wasn't just my own experience. It was the narrative I'd grown up with, despite the love songs playing through Dad's speakers in the living room. Both sets of my grandparents were divorced. My parents had been separated several times. And both of my dad's siblings were divorced.

Maybe love simply didn't last. Maybe like a gallon of milk it had an expiration date. And when that date came and went it was time to throw it out, because spoiled milk smells to high heaven and makes me nauseous.

But in Psalm 136 the psalmist disagrees with my college-aged thesis. The psalmist declares that there is a love that never expires. It's bigger and better than the love described in love songs. Psalm 136 states twenty-six times that God's love endures—forever.

To prove his point, the psalmist starts giving examples of how God's love has gone on and on and on. The psalmist says, "Remember when God made the heavens? When He made the earth and water? When He created light—the sun, the moon, the stars?" (see vv. 5–9). The writer continues, "Oh yeah, and remember when God led our people out of slavery in Egypt? Remember when He divided the Red Sea for us and then let it swoosh back over Pharaoh and destroyed his whole army? Oh, and then after that it was God who struck down the mighty kings who were against us."

The psalmist even rattles off some of the kings by name. He recites multiple ways that God was there for His people over hundreds of years, how God provided for, protected, and came through for the Israelites, how thoroughly and faithfully God loved them. And with each statement of God's goodness, the echoing refrain in this psalm is "His love endures forever."

We can do the same.

Ready? Let's do this together.

Start with creation. What are some of your favorite parts?

I'll go.

Give thanks to the Lord for He created the intoxicating scent of lavender. He made scarlet maple leaves that flutter to the ground in the fall. He gave the ocean its mighty roar. He handcrafted graceful deer with soft brown eyes and fur the color of their surroundings, an organic camouflage to keep them safe.

His love endures forever.

Remember to put that phrase at the end of your

statement about creation. It's a punctuation mark to remind us of what God has done, of how He's been faithful
throughout the world's story and our own story, of how
much He loves us.

Okay, next think of something in your family history
you can thank God for. Not something you remember
but something that's been handed down to you, either
an old photo, a story one of your grandparents shared,
or even a family tree you discovered on yellowing pages
tucked in the front of an old family Bible.

This is mine: Give thanks to Him who enabled Cynthia
Erskine (that's my great-grandma) to purchase a parcel
of land in Florida that she willed to my mom when she
passed away and that my mom then sold, putting the
proceeds in a savings account that paid for my college
education.

His love endures forever.
What's yours?

The psalmist ends the psalm with some general statements.

> He remembered us in our low estate
> *His love endures forever.*
> and freed us from our enemies.
> *His love endures forever.*
> He gives food to every creature.
> *His love endures forever.* (vv. 23–25)

There have certainly been times I was in a "low estate,"
that I was sad or lonely or scared or worried, and God was
there for me. The times He guided me safely home while
I drove at night in a storm, clutching the steering wheel.
The days when I had four kids eight years old and under
and I couldn't remember the last time I'd slept through the
night. God gave me daily endurance and energy to take
another trip to the park or to cut colorful construction

paper to create another craft. There were the days when I was freed from my enemies—when a meeting with an angry coworker ended early, when I dreaded making a phone call to someone abrasive and the call rolled into their voice mail, when the child who was terrorizing our playgroup (translation: my kiddos) simply stopped coming. You know your moments when you were low too. And times God saved you from enemies. And perhaps a time when someone provided you with a meal. Thank Him for those things. Remember those things.

His love endures forever.

There's something beautiful about giving thanks. When we do, it reminds us of God's unfailing love. I find the more I give thanks, the more I want to give thanks. As I'm writing this chapter, I'm thinking, Oh yeah, and thank you, God, for my incredible great-aunt who paid for my mom's education, so my mom would think it was important for me to have one. And thank you for keeping my son safe in that car accident, for giving my daughter the courage to break up with the boy who wasn't right for her, for literally putting all the pieces in place for my other daughter's job. You did all that! I remember when I had my third baby and it was December and so bitter cold; I was fearful of leaving the house with her, and a friend brought over a giant fruit tray. And although we had groceries, that fresh fruit all cut up was exactly what I was craving. It felt like a beam of sunshine in our house—the most delicious treat I could imagine. I can still taste the sweet pineapple on my tongue. Once you get me going, I can ramble for quite a while about the blessings God in His never-ending love has bestowed upon me. I bet you can to. But first we have to start.

If you ever question if you could be loved, if anyone truly loves you, take a moment to assess all that God has done and is doing for you. It's such a testament to what true love looks like.

It turns out an endless, faithful love that lasts longer than the rhymes of poets and the perfume of clover, and any romance or relationship we could find on earth, does exist. It's right here for the taking. For all of us.

The twelfth of never might have been intended as a catchy phrase for a sappy love song, but it actually makes a pretty good description for God's love. It doesn't just last a lifetime. It doesn't just last until some imaginary date. God's love? It endures forever.

> Give thanks to the God of heaven.
> *His love endures forever.* (v. 26)

RESTORE

Go through the prompts in this chapter and write your own psalm of thanks to the Lord. Make sure to add "His love endures forever" after each phrase or point of thanks. I find it extra impactful to read it out loud.

28

YOU INSPIRE AWE

Psalm 139

*You have searched me, L*ORD*,*
  and you know me.
You know when I sit and when I rise;
  you perceive my thoughts from afar.
You discern my going out and my lying down;
  you are familiar with all my ways.
Before a word is on my tongue
  *you, L*ORD*, know it completely.*
You hem me in behind and before,
  and you lay your hand upon me.
Such knowledge is too wonderful for me,
  too lofty for me to attain.

Where can I go from your Spirit?
  Where can I flee from your presence?
If I go up to the heavens, you are there;
  if I make my bed in the depths, you are
    there.
If I rise on the wings of the dawn,
  if I settle on the far side of the sea,
even there your hand will guide me,
  your right hand will hold me fast.
If I say, "Surely the darkness will hide me
  and the light become night around me,"
even the darkness will not be dark to you;
  the night will shine like the day,
  for darkness is as light to you.

For you created my inmost being;
you knit me together in my mother's womb.
I praise you because I am fearfully and won-
derfully made;
your works are wonderful,
I know that full well.
My frame was not hidden from you
when I was made in the secret place,
when I was woven together in the depths
of the earth.
Your eyes saw my unformed body;
all the days ordained for me were written
in your book
before one of them came to be.
How precious to me are your thoughts, God!
How vast is the sum of them!
Were I to count them,
they would outnumber the grains of
sand—
when I awake, I am still with you.

If only you, God, would slay the wicked!
Away from me, you who are bloodthirsty!
They speak of you with evil intent;
your adversaries misuse your name.
Do I not hate those who hate you, LORD,
and abhor those who are in rebellion
against you?
I have nothing but hatred for them;
I count them my enemies.
Search me, God, and know my heart;
test me and know my anxious thoughts.
See if there is any offensive way in me,
and lead me in the way everlasting.

We were in between formal Bible studies at church, but there were four of us who were really craving

God's Word and community, so we committed to getting together on our own. It was super informal. No videos or study book. No assignments. No agenda. We sat outside by a pond in the back of one of the women's yards. On a blessedly sunny, bright, and breezy-for-early-November-in-Ohio day we started by closing our eyes and breathing, finding some stillness. Then we prayed that we'd tune out distractions to be more aware of God's presence. I offered one verse to meditate on and let the conversation flow.

> But you are a chosen people, a royal priesthood, a holy nation, God's special possession, that you may declare the praises of him who called you out of darkness into his wonderful light. (1 Peter 2:9)

I asked my friends the same thing God had asked me when He placed this verse in front of me earlier in the week: "How are you doing with walking around in these promises—that you're chosen, royal, and holy, God's prized possession?"

My friends looked down. I know these women. We've been faithfully meeting and intimately sharing despite a pretty strange set of circumstances. Still, they wouldn't meet my gaze. I waited.

Finally, one of them spoke. "I have a hard time believing that."

"You mean you don't believe it? Or it's just hard to hold on to?" I probed.

"I have days I fully believe it and feel it." She smiled. I could see on her face how she felt when she believed it, so completely loved. "But most days it's just hard to believe that I am actually that valuable."

The other ladies nodded.

So did I.

These words are in the Bible, the Word of God, so I

acknowledge them as truth. As an author, I always like to know who wrote what I'm reading, get a bit of their backstory. The author of these words is Peter. As in Peter the disciple who lived with, studied under, and followed Jesus around for three years. Peter who was an uneducated fisherman. Peter who knew Jesus so intimately. And yet Peter denied Jesus out loud, not once but three times on the day Jesus most needed a friend: crucifixion day. Peter knew down to his core that even though he was poor and flawed, Jesus chose him. That even after he turned his back on Jesus in His darkest hour, Jesus still considered him chosen, holy, royal, and prized. Peter wanted to make sure we know it as well.

Do you?

Do you walk around feeling like royalty—like you have all the power and authority and privilege of our one true king, Jesus? Acting like you're holy—set apart by God for a special purpose? Holding dear in your heart that Jesus chose you and considers you His prized possession?

It's not just Peter who understood how Christ sees us, who we truly are. Centuries prior to Peter's letter, King David understood who He was in God. He writes in Psalm 139:13–16:

> For you created my inmost being;
>   you knit me together in my mother's
>   womb.
> I praise you because I am fearfully and won-
>   derfully made;
>   your works are wonderful,
>   I know that full well.
> My frame was not hidden from you
>   when I was made in the secret place,
>   when I was woven together in the depths
>   of the earth.
> Your eyes saw my unformed body;

all the days ordained for me were written
in your book
before one of them came to be.

I love the imagery of being knit together. I picture God
with His almighty knitting needles. If you've ever knit or
cross-stitched or even tried to mend a hole in your favorite sweatpants, you know that each stitch is intentional.
You have to select the yarn or thread and wrap it around
or thread it through your needle, which takes precision
and concentration. You have to consider where you'll
place the needle, how much you'll move it. And that was
all for *one* stitch. As God created your nose and your
left elbow, your laugh and your sigh, your desires and
motivations, the way you relate to others, how tall you
are, how long or short your toes are, whether numbers
all in a row soothe you or you'd rather string together
beads or words, whether you prefer to do things with
your mind or your hands—as He formed each of those
things He intentionally considered that stitch and then
the next one. And when He was done—God declared
you a wonderful creation!

You may have heard this phrase "fearfully and wonderfully made" before—maybe seen it on a cute graphic
tee or mug. But did you know the original Hebrew word
for "fearfully" has nothing to do with fright? It means "to
be in awe of." Like how you would walk into a throne
room and be in awe of the king. You would be *fearful*,
not scared but reverent, starstruck. And the Bible says
this is how God created you. To inspire awe.

When a passage in the Bible resonates with me, I like
to read it in multiple versions. Here are the same verses
from *The Message*:

Oh yes, you shaped me first inside, then out;
you formed me in my mother's womb.

235

I thank you, High God—you're breathtaking!
  Body and soul, I am marvelously made!
  I worship in adoration—what a creation!
You know me inside and out,
    you know every bone in my body;
You know exactly how I was made, bit by
      bit,
    how I was sculpted from nothing into
      something.
Like an open book, you watched me grow
    from conception to birth;
    all the stages of my life were spread out
      before you,
The days of my life all prepared
    before I'd even lived one day.

The psalmist actually worships God for making him so awesome! King David says of himself, "What a creation!" but not in a haughty way, because David continues, "I was sculpted from nothing." David is worshipping God for the way God created him.

Do you do that?

Do you thank God for giving you your body? Your intellect? Your emotions? Your tendencies? Your strengths *and* your weaknesses?

It seems the main reason we struggle to believe these truths is that we measure ourselves against the wrong standards:

1. Worldly standards

2. Fictitious standards

3. Standards of perfection

All of which are ridiculous if we admit them out loud.

One of the ladies from our informal Bible study admitted to being harsh on herself if she's out of any type of food, even though she has a full pantry with plenty of choices for her family.

Another said she feels guilty if she ever does anything that pulls her out of her home in the evenings—a time she has committed for family.

Ugh. I also deduct points on my mental sticker chart for both those things. Our group also admitted to feeling like we need to have constantly clean homes, one-hundred-percent happy kids, and explain or validate what we do with our time (these came from both stay-at-home moms and those who had jobs outside the house). The expectations my group was trying to live up to were impossible or fictitious.

And if someone does expect us to have three types of granola bars and four fresh fruit choices and be one-hundred-percent available all the time to everyone while maintaining a perfect household and completing our work—they are being unreasonable. One woman I know puts exorbitant pressure on herself to earn more money even though she and her husband are financially stable. Yet another feels pressure to entertain—to host playdates for her littles, holiday gatherings for her family, book clubs, small groups, cookouts for colleagues, all at her home and all with recipes and party vibes that Joanna Gaines would approve of. Another has a need to approach everything with a unique spin—from the meals she makes to the work she does to the outfits she chooses. She exhausts herself in the attempt to always be original.

None of these things are bad things. Wanting to have welcoming homes and a happy family and financial stability, to do our creative best, to be present for the people we love? These are all awesome things! It's not the wanting that's the issue. It's the judging our self-worth by how well we do or do not accomplish these things instead of by the fact that God created us and loves us that's the problem.

Are you striving for any of those things?

When you fail to meet those standards, how do you feel about yourself?

We believers are God's prized possessions. God knit us together stitch by stitch. He declares us wonderful and awe-inspiring. Not if we achieve a list of things. Not if we perform those things well. But simply because He made us. Just because we're His kids. There is no louder applause than the applause of heaven. There is no sweeter sound than Jesus telling us He loves us.

Yet we trade those beautiful, life-giving affirmations for the hollow, shallow praise of this world. I don't want to anymore.

You?

How do we change the way we see ourselves? How do we cling to the truth of who Jesus says we are?

1. Saturate ourselves in the truths of the Bible. The more we read and reflect on them, the louder they'll become in our minds and hearts. We'll be better able to drown out the noise of the world with the truths that we are royal, holy, prized, awe-inspiring, and wonderful.

2. Hang out with people who point us back to those truths. Spending a couple of hours every other week with my Bible study women does this for me. We talk about where we're struggling. We remind each other who we truly are. Whose we truly are. Who God really is. What that means for us. We pray for one another. We look each other in the eyes and ask penetrating questions and speak beautiful encouragement. I drive away feeling more royal, holy, prized, and awe-inspiring than on the way there. Every time.

3. Do the things God calls us specifically to do. David mentions in verse 16, "All the days

ordained for me were written in your book before one of them came to be." God ordained us to do important work for His kingdom. If you are great at organizing things, perhaps God has designed you to organize your church's giving tree or the school's food drive. Maybe He's called you to use your skills to run a giant organization ethically or to plan weddings, blessing every bride and groom who meet with you. If God gave you a heart for kiddos, maybe He'll call you to babysit, nanny, own a day care, or volunteer at an after-school program for underprivileged kids. For me it's writing. For one of the ladies in my Bible study it's beekeeping. Another is going to seminary. Yet another is moving to Japan for her husband's job and hopes to share the love of Jesus in a culture where few know Him. And another is a stay-at-home mama to two adorable toddlers. That's just our group of five! If any of us switched roles we'd feel clunky and ill-equipped. Let's just say I'd make a horrible beekeeper. But when we do the things God calls us to do, well, we feel more like His prized possessions.

I want to trade in the false expectations I put on myself for the glorious exaltations God gives me. I want to stop worrying about what others think and lean into Christ's love and acceptance. I want to stop putting pressure on myself with make-believe standards and instead do the good work God has written into His book for me.

Will you join me?

Because you inspire awe! You are a child of the one true King. You were intentionally knit stitch by stitch by the Creator of the universe. It's time to live like it.

—— RESTORE ——

Where do you struggle to fully believe that you are wonderful?

Commit to trying the three steps listed in the chapter this week:

1. Spend some time in the Bible every day. Reading Psalm 139 every day this week would be a wonderful place to start.

2. Schedule a coffee date, walk, or video chat with a friend who celebrates who you are in Christ. If you don't have a friend like this, consider who you know who lives in the truth that they are wonderfully made. Ask them if they have fifteen minutes to chat about how they live out that mindset.

3. Do something you know you're good at. It could be creating a spreadsheet, repairing a broken appliance, designing a graphic, or simmering a pot of soup. You know what these things are.

Take time to journal and talk to God about how you felt about yourself after all three of these activities.

29

NARNIAN WOODS

Psalm 145

I will exalt you, my God the King;
I will praise your name for ever and ever.
Every day I will praise you
and extol your name for ever and ever.

Great is the LORD and most worthy of praise;
his greatness no one can fathom.
One generation commends your works to
another;
they tell of your mighty acts.
They speak of the glorious splendor of your
majesty—
and I will meditate on your wonderful
works.
They tell of the power of your awesome
works—
and I will proclaim your great deeds.
They celebrate your abundant goodness
and joyfully sing of your righteousness.

The LORD is gracious and compassionate,
slow to anger and rich in love.

The LORD is good to all;
he has compassion on all he has made.
All your works praise you, LORD;
your faithful people extol you.

They tell of the glory of your kingdom
  and speak of your might,
so that all people may know of your mighty
      acts
  and the glorious splendor of your
      kingdom.
Your kingdom is an everlasting kingdom,
  and your dominion endures through all
      generations.

The LORD *is trustworthy in all he promises*
  and faithful in all he does.
The LORD *upholds all who fall*
  and lifts up all who are bowed down.
The eyes of all look to you,
  and you give them their food at the proper
      time.
You open your hand
  and satisfy the desires of every living thing.

The LORD *is righteous in all his ways*
  and faithful in all he does.
The LORD *is near to all who call on him,*
  to all who call on him in truth.
He fulfills the desires of those who fear him;
  he hears their cry and saves them.
The LORD *watches over all who love him,*
  but all the wicked he will destroy.

My mouth will speak in praise of the LORD.
  Let every creature praise his holy name
  for ever and ever.

"I t truly was like walking through Narnia with you today,"
my friend Beth exclaimed as we approached the parking
lot adjacent to the wooded trail we'd been walking.
  I'd been thinking the exact same thing since the moment
I stepped onto the trailhead. The quiet that a snowfall

brings, beautifully covering every branch of every tree in the woods with a layer of sparkly white frosting. It felt like the part in *The Lion, The Witch and the Wardrobe* where Lucy hides in a wardrobe while playing hide-and-seek with her siblings and discovers, instead of the wooden back of the wardrobe she expected, a path in the woods, snow gently crunching under her feet.

"Except we tackled some really hard stuff," Beth said. "Maybe God gave us this beautiful snow globe so we could deal with the heaviness." She spread out her mittened hands, embracing the thick flakes tumbling from the sky.

"There was plenty of hard stuff in Narnia." I smiled, recalling images from one of my favorite book series—evil witches and queens, manipulative apes, untrustworthy dwarves, and corrupt uncles. But my smile wasn't because of the wickedness; it was because love and goodness always conquered the evil in the end of the magical tales penned by C. S. Lewis. I was also smiling considering how the heroes and heroines of each of the seven books always had a companion to help them navigate away from the darkness and toward the light. Because it's tricky to figure out on your own.

Psalm 145 talks about how powerful it is to have traveling companions on this journey of life. It talks about believers speaking together of God's wonderful and awesome works, His abundant goodness, focusing on God's light.

> [Your people] tell of the glory of your kingdom
> and speak of your might,
> so that all people may know of your mighty
> acts
> and the glorious splendor of your king-
> dom. (vv. 11–12)

Beth is this for me—one of the companions who helps me navigate away from the darkness in the world and in my life and toward the light. By talking about the glorious splendor of God's kingdom and His mighty acts, by celebrating God's strength together, we're reminded of who He is and what He can do. The darkness pales. I believe God puts people like this in our lives so that we can better blaze the trails of this world.

Just on this one walk Beth and I marveled at a bunny's tiny footprints fresh in the snow, shared some ugly, painful history that has left generational scars on both of our family trees, discussed our plans for Christmas, and bounced ideas for new work projects off each other. It's all there in all our lives—the celebrations and the sorrows. The everyday and the extraordinary. In Narnia there was both the nefarious White Witch's castle, stunning from the outside but cold and terrifying within, *and* Cair Paravel, the lovely palace by the sea where Aslan crowned good and noble kings and queens to rule the kingdom with care and respect.

Because God created the world and us who dwell in it, because He loves us, His creations, there will always be grace and light and hope. But because the enemy also lurks in this world, trying to dilute the reality of God's great love for us, when hard things come—and they will come—we can get distracted from the pure light Jesus offers and stumble around in the darkness. We can become like Edmund, a confused child who heads through the snowy woods to the wicked White Witch's castle, seeking the warmth and Turkish delight the witch promised but never delivered.

But just like Aslan (the lion who represents Christ in Lewis's allegorical tales) always seems to show up in the darkest chapters of the Narnia adventures, God watches over all who love Him, as David tells us in Psalm 145:

> The LORD is trustworthy in all he promises
> and faithful in all he does.

The LORD upholds all who fall
    and lifts up all who are bowed down.
The eyes of all look to you,
    and you give them their food at the proper
        time.
You open your hand
    and satisfy the desires of every living thing.
      (vv. 13–16)

This is our God. A God who is faithful when even our families let us down. A God who picks us back up when we land flat on our faces. A God who satisfies our true desires—our core, deep-down heart's desires. And a God who gives us other humans to help us decipher where to turn, what to grab on to, what to let go of, when to head back, and what our true desires actually are, as well as what's getting in the way of us being fulfilled.

Sure, we sometimes figure these out by ourselves. Often through prayer and reading the Bible God directs us to the truth that lights up our paths. But friendship is yet another one of God's marvelous gifts, another facet of how He loves us—that He provides us with fellow sojourners so we can ask, "Does that path look like the right way? Or do you think it's a trap?" Then our companion can tell us, "I know that person seems friendly, but actually they have *their* best interests in mind, not *yours*." Or maybe they'll remind us not to give up, or that we are loved, or that someone is cheering us on.

King David, the author of this psalm, had a best friend named Jonathan. Jonathan stood up for David when King Saul talked badly about him, encouraged David's faith in God, wept with him, gave David a military tunic and sword to protect him in battle, and helped David escape from furious King Saul. The friendship of David and Jonathan was like that of brothers: "As soon as he had finished speaking to Saul, the soul of Jonathan was knit to the soul of David, and Jonathan loved him as his own soul" (1 Samuel 18:1 ESV).

In the beginning God created Eve for Adam so he wouldn't be alone. God knew we would need people. Good, faithful, caring people who love us well, cry with us, look out for us, and point us back to God, helping us live our lives more fully. Jesus also patterned this kind of friendship for us. Jesus spent the last three years of His life with the twelve men we call the disciples—eating, praying, walking, teaching, and doing life with them.

Beth and I discussed a heartbreaking crisis of a loved one. Neither of us knew how to solve their problem or what words might be healing for them or which actions might help or comfort them, but we were able to agree that God knew exactly what this person needed most. So we prayed in the middle of the trail, delicate, icy snowflakes tickling our noses. We prayed that God would satisfy this wounded loved one and give them exactly what they needed in their time of trial—their "food at the proper time" (Psalm 145:15).

And in the next breath we praised God, as David does at the beginning of this psalm, because it was so dang gorgeous outside. Although Beth and I were talking about deep, painful things, we couldn't get over the winter wonderland we were walking through and our magnificent God who created it all and allowed us to stroll through this magical forest. (Okay, trail through the woods one mile from my neighborhood in Ohio, but in the moment it was every bit a magical forest.)

> Every day I will praise you
>> and extol your name for ever and ever. . . .
>
> One generation commends your works to
>> another;
>> they tell of your mighty acts.

> They speak of the glorious splendor of your
> majesty—
> and I will meditate on your wonderful
> works. (vv. 2, 4–5)

Then I told Beth something brave I'd recently done. And about a wonderful writing opportunity God had hand delivered to me. And she shared the fun she'd experienced recently moderating a panel of female entrepreneurs and the meal she prepared, complete with creamy, cheesy twice-baked potatoes, for her wedding anniversary. Plus we chatted about who we thought would win *The Voice*, because even though neither of us watch much TV, we both are addicted to this show.

This is what the psalmist is trying to convey. Even though life is full of ups and downs, daily joys, and long-term struggles, our faithful God, who is "gracious and compassionate, slow to anger and rich in love" (v. 8), is with us through it all—both the friendly talking mice *and* the giants who want to eat us for dinner. Or if you don't live in Narnia (sigh), the Lord is with us when the scars from our family histories flare up *and* when we accomplish something meaningful at work *and* when we're not sure how to intervene or not intervene when our kids are constantly bickering. Our God, who is good and compassionate to all (v. 9), is generous to provide us with people who help us turn away from the evil lurking on our path and toward the beautiful castles He's prepared for us.

I love Jesus and all He does for me. When I walk alone in the woods, I often find myself talking to Him, asking Him questions, praising Him. But how beautiful that in addition to being my very best friend, Jesus has also given me earthly friends, like Beth, who show me even more dimensions of His goodness, more ways He's on the move, more prayers He's answering, more insights of His wisdom. That on this day, on this picturesque, wintery walk where the air felt hushed and my heart felt full, I understood this psalm at a deeper level, understood God better, because of Beth.

RESTORE

Do you have someone who helps you see God better? Who steers you toward light and away from darkness?

If so, reach out to them today. Give them a call, schedule a walk or a coffee date, or invite them over to dinner.

If not, start the search. This isn't as daunting as it sounds. God wants you to be surrounded by good people. It delights Him when you find a faithful friend or two who point you back to Jesus. Church is a great place to start. Does the church you attend or one in your community have a group for singles? Widows? Professionals? Whatever life stage you're in? Or maybe there's someone who you know loves Jesus and you've been meaning to get to know them . . . Now's your chance.

30

EVERY DAY

Psalm 150

Praise the LORD.

Praise God in his sanctuary;
*   praise him in his mighty heavens.*
Praise him for his acts of power;
*   praise him for his surpassing greatness.*
Praise him with the sounding of the trumpet,
*   praise him with the harp and lyre,*
praise him with timbrel and dancing,
*   praise him with the strings and pipe,*
praise him with the clash of cymbals,
*   praise him with resounding cymbals.*

Let everything that has breath praise the LORD.

Praise the LORD.

We've traveled the pages of this book together, exploring what talking to God looks and feels like, what it does for our lives. We've discussed that God wants us to talk to Him about everything.

Every.

Single.

Thing.

He wants us to praise Him when we make it to our meeting on time and when the wedding bells ring and when we have the most delicious piece of avocado toast with a drizzle of olive oil and a light sprinkle of sea salt on top. God wants us to cry out in disgust when we witness racism and injustice. God wants us to bring our tears to Him when we feel physical or emotional pain. And He wants us to bring our fears to Him so He can dismantle them. We see all these emotions expressed to God throughout the Psalms.

That's what the Psalms are—prayers of God's people written into songs, conversations with their Creator about all the things they experienced and encountered. The good and bad. The easy and hard. The surprises and the predictable. We've also chatted about why this matters, about how praying flips a switch inside of us and allows us to see things from His perspective. Which, sidenote, is always more accurate and complete than ours. And always involves Him loving us.

Psalm 150 wraps up our thirty-chapter discussion about what happens when we spend more time talking to God, thrilling on His words. We praise Him.

The psalmist says:

> Praise the LORD.
>
> Praise God in his sanctuary;
>   praise him in his mighty heavens.
> Praise him for his acts of power;
>   praise him for his surpassing greatness.
>   (vv. 1–2)

That's a lot of praising. But think of all we've learned. Goodness, it seems like the least we can do after we've talked about how faithful and personal our God is. He answers requests we don't even know we should ask for, stands by us even when no one else does, energizes and fuels and protects and restores us. So, yes! Praise God for His surpassing greatness.

The psalmist continues:

> Praise him with the sounding of the trumpet,
>> praise him with the harp and lyre,
> praise him with timbrel and dancing,
>> praise him with the strings and pipe,
> praise him with the clash of cymbals,
>> praise him with resounding cymbals.
>
> (vv. 3–5)

Basically the psalmist is saying to praise God with everything you've got, with anything you have handy, with all the things you can think of. With brass instruments, string instruments, percussion, and woodwinds. Not just with cymbals but with resounding cymbals. Not just with instruments but also with dancing.

If you're a musician this might get you excited. But not all of us are. I kind-of-sort-of play the piano and can't sing a note. I mean, I do sing loads of notes, but rarely on key. I adore music and actually have my grandfather's silver trumpet that I don't even know how to hold properly in a case in a closet. But I don't think that's the psalmist's point.

So what do these verses mean for you and me? Take a moment to scan your life. What do you touch during the day? What sounds do you make? How can you use those things to praise the Lord?

For me, I almost daily touch lunch boxes and laundry and laptop keys. How can I use those things to praise the Lord? I can whisper a prayer of thanks to God for my kids as I pull their lunch boxes out of the fridge in the morning so they'll remember to take them to school. I can spend my time folding laundry listening to worship music, thanking God for clothes and for sunshine streaming through our windows as I sing along in my head or possibly out loud. I can ask for God's guidance as I sit down to write each day—that the words and stories He gives me can be used for His glory, to point people back to Him. These are ways I can take the things in my life— *all* the things—and praise Him.

How about you?

Paul explains this process of praising God all the time to the church in Rome like this: "So here's what I want you to do, God helping you: Take your everyday, ordinary life—your sleeping, eating, going-to-work, and walking-around life—and place it before God as an offering" (Romans 12:1 MSG).

Your walking-around life.

As you drag the trash can to the curb. As you plug in your phone to charge. As you unload the groceries from your trunk. Praise the Lord—for sanitation workers and communication and food. Or maybe for the really nice message someone left on your voice mail or the twittering of birds in the branches overhead or the fact that it's Friday. In your everyday, ordinary life, dance while you're chopping veggies or climbing the stairs to your apartment. Sing while you're loading paper into the printer or typing in your password or cleaning up your workstation. Let all that you do praise the Lord.

Yes, some days the praise will come easier than others. That day when it truly feels like spring for the first time, when the air is warm and smells like things are growing right out of the ground. When you have dinner plans at the hip brick-oven pizza joint with one of your favorite humans. Getting ready, you slide on your cute boots and can almost taste the melted brie with honey appetizer. From your awesome parking spot you can already smell the woodsy smoke from the brick oven. Praise the Lord!

And there will be days when it feels impossible to praise the Lord. The days in the middle of winter when your depression is at its peak, as dark and gray as the sky. When there's a chill permeating your home and you can feel it in your heart too. When someone you were counting on lets you down. When a wound from the past is festering. When the fridge is empty and your account balance is low. And no one seems to be listening.

But God is listening.

And He sees you.

And He loves you. And even on this day, like when the psalmists were overtaken in battle by their enemies, you can still praise God, because even if no one else seems to notice or care, the God who created you does. He sees it all and He aches with you and He longs to comfort you. He will be your refuge.

My son leads worship at church and at a scattering of other gatherings on his campus. We have great chats about worship—about what it means, what it looks like, what its purpose is. And we always land on this: "Worship is simply acknowledging how great God is. It's praising Him."

Yes, my son does that with the strum of his guitar and raspy voice and melodious chords on the keyboard. And he'll even do it in front of large groups of people with the intent of pointing them to God's goodness.

But he looks at me and says, "You lead people to worship too."

And I grin because I hope that's what's happened here. I pray that God used this book to point you to His goodness. That you've found yourself praising God as you've read. That just like the psalmist finishing the last song on the last page of the book of Psalms, your thought as you finish this last page is, "Let everything that has breath praise the LORD. Praise the LORD" (150:6).

RESTORE

Set a timer for five minutes and spend the whole time praising God.

Spend some time asking God how you can incorporate more praise into your everyday, ordinary, walking-around life.

ACKNOWLEDGMENTS

The flip-flopped thing about being a writer is that although I spend hours in my writing nook alone with a heap of books, several Bibles, a pad of sticky notes, pens, coffee, water, and my laptop, I cannot write without the life and people outside of my nook. And for them I'm forever grateful.

This book wouldn't be possible without the psalmists who put their heart's cries on paper centuries ago. I am daily blessed by the words they wrote and the songs they composed. Their psalms help me see God more clearly, help me better bring all myself to Him, so that I can better understand all that He is for me.

Jesus, you are so faithful, loving, and kind. Thank you for giving me this opportunity to write about your steadfast love that endures forever. Thank you for hemming me in, picking me up, reminding me that I am fearfully and wonderfully made, standing over me like a watchman, leading me to green pastures, and restoring my soul.

Brett, thank you for being the person who best demonstrates God's relentless, unselfish love to me. Every day I thank Jesus that I get to be your wife and do this life with you.

Maddie, Max, Mallory, and Maguire, I see God's

goodness, His provision to me, His unfailing love in each of you. Thank you for being you—your wonderfully made selves—and for filling my days with laughter and love.

Bob Hostetler, you are the ultimate agent. I am beyond grateful for your guidance, patience, expertise, and support.

Amy Parker, how could I ever thank you? You've been with me since the first page of my first book (and every page since), cheering me on, listening to everything about my life, eating chocolate, drinking coffee, listening to music with me, and being the dearest friend.

Tammy Bundy, thank you for reading the first draft of this book, for all your writing and life encouragement, and mostly for your friendship.

Beth Troy, thank you for walks in the woods, friendship, and community. You are an incredible gift to me.

Thank you to everyone on the team at Our Daily Bread who makes me feel like family and turns my ideas into beautiful books. Specifically, Dawn Anderson, thank you for championing this project on the Psalms and giving me the opportunity to write it. Joel Armstrong, you make my writing clearer, more accurate, stronger, and all around infinitely better. Thank you! Bill Crowder, I'm honored by your wisdom. John van der Veen, you positively rock! Patti Brinks, thank you for the lovely cover. I am honored to partner with all of you in sharing the good news of Jesus.

APPENDIX:
HEARING GOD

I talk a lot in this book about hearing God or God telling me something. What exactly does that mean? How do we hear God's voice?

Like a good Father with His kids, God speaks to us in many ways. I communicate with my kids in a variety of ways—audible conversations, texts (of words or pictures), phone calls, video chats, notes I write, hugs, eye rolls, an elbow jab, or that look across the table that will most likely cause us both to burst into laughter. Or the look that tells one of my kids "Stop!" or "No!" without a single word. I also "speak" to my kids by showing up at their games, listening when they need to talk, doing one of their chores for them on a day they're overwhelmed, or making their favorite meal or dessert. I might drop a comment on one of their social media posts or brag about them on mine.

There's no question between my kids and me that these all count as them hearing from me. One of the important things to realize about "hearing from God" is that we have to be open-minded to the myriad of ways this could happen.

In chapter 1 we talked about the Bible being God's Word, about thrilling on it. When we read the Bible we get to hear God's words firsthand. Which on any given day might excite, motivate, strengthen, convict, encourage, or calm us. Some days we won't feel anything, but as God told the prophet Isaiah, His words always achieve a purpose.

> My word . . . goes out from my mouth:
>   It will not return to me empty,
> but will accomplish what I desire
>   and achieve the purpose for which I sent it.
>   (Isaiah 55:11)

We don't always see that purpose, but God plants His words in our hearts. Maybe for a later time or place. Maybe to begin showing us something that will take a while for us to understand. Maybe to divert our attention away from a lie or distraction in our life. Some days the words on the pages of our Bibles might leap out at us, as if they were especially written for us on that specific day.

Let me give you an example.

I was going through a Bible study with a group of women. One of our assignments in our workbook was to read a passage in Jeremiah 1. I ended up reading the whole chapter because I felt the urge to go ahead and read it all. These verses weren't my assigned reading, but that day I read them.

> "You must go to everyone I send you to and say whatever I command you. Do not be afraid of them, for I am with you and will rescue you," declares the LORD.
>   Then the LORD reached out his hand and touched my mouth and said to me, "I have put my words in your mouth." (vv. 7–9)

God spoke this message to the prophet Jeremiah. But on that day, it felt like God was speaking it to *me*. I was scheduled to speak at a women's conference that weekend and was feeling a bit nervous. God's words to Jeremiah got me all excited: "You must go to everyone I send you to and say whatever I command you. . . . I have put my words in your mouth."

I thanked God for giving me the words He wanted me to say, for putting this passage in front of me on this day. And as I was praying, I felt another nudge, this time to share these verses with my friend who was also speaking at the event. I snapped a picture of the page in my Bible with my phone and texted it to Shena, who said it was exactly the encouragement she needed to hear.

Shena in turn read the whole chapter and saw something a few verses down that she felt God telling her to share with a mutual friend of ours, Allison. Shena sent those verses to Allison, who said those words spoke directly to her. It was wild. And awesome. And that's how the Bible might speak to you. Through something you're directed to read. Something you read on your own. Or something a friend sends you. God could do any of the above and so much more.

Prayer is another way we hear from God. It's a direct conversation with Him. Like all conversations, it's two-way. One where we can praise God and tell Him everything that's on our minds and hearts. And one where we can listen to His responses. Sometimes we feel an answer from God during prayer—that inner tug that seems to be a direct response to what we asked or said. This could be a word, sentence, feeling, or picture.

Maybe you're asking God to calm you down because you're so worked up about something someone said to you. Your prayer sounds more like a rant than a prayer, and then you feel an overwhelming sense of peace. That's God answering you. You weren't feeling peaceful at all, and then you suddenly were.

Or maybe the sentence "Let it go" appears in your mind.

Hmm. You hadn't been thinking about letting this go. You were dwelling on it, thank you very much. It doesn't feel like this is your thought but more like the thought of a God who loves you and doesn't want you to wallow, of a God who also loves the person who said that thing.

But how do you know if it was or wasn't God? Well, does it sound like something God would say? Is it biblical? In this case, yes. God tells us to love our neighbors (Mark 12:31) and wants us to cast all our cares on Him (1 Peter 5:7). Letting go of this grudge so we can better love this person and casting it at the feet of Jesus so it won't fester in us sounds very much like something God would suggest. But if you have an urge to post something nasty about that person on social media, that does *not* sound like how Jesus instructs us to live.

Sometimes we pray and pray and struggle to hear God. As I write this appendix, I've been asking God something very specific for months. I don't seem to be getting any suggestions, hints, or ideas from Him. Nothing in the Bible has jumped out at me about this issue. But I'm still praying and still reading my Bible. Because I know reading His words will not return void (Isaiah 55:11). I know that continuing to talk to Him through prayer is purposeful and important (1 Thessalonians 5:16–18). I'm confident He will give me direction. I know that our God is faithful.

We need to remember to be patient, me especially. Because God isn't a vending machine, where we pop in a prayer and get out an answer. If there's something we need to know, God will tell us when the time is right.

My friends Amanda and Lauren know this. They were both seniors in college who had secured jobs in Columbus, Ohio. Separately they'd been praying for a roommate. But the clock to graduation was ticking and they still didn't have someone to split the rent with in their new city.

I'd gotten to know both girls during their college careers, and before they graduated I wanted to see each of them one more time. I met Lauren at the park and listened as she explained her roommate dilemma and asked for prayers. When a few days later Amanda mentioned her same situation, this question popped out of my mouth before I could even process it: "Do you know Lauren?"

It was crazy. Both Amanda and Lauren were entrepreneurship majors and Spanish minors. Both sang in the worship band at our church. Still, they barely knew each other. But I knew them both, and God used me to introduce them, providing the roommate they'd been praying about, an answer to their prayers not during prayer but through a woman (me) they mutually knew. Not as soon as they'd hoped for an answer, but in time for them to find an apartment together. God speaks to us in so many ways.

Songs, sermons, books, movies, and podcasts are all ways God might talk to us. When we're reading or listening they might speak directly to our soul, to the thing we were wrestling with. This is often God speaking to you. Again, ask yourself, Does it sound like God would say it? Is it biblical? These are great litmus tests.

Sometimes I hear God when I'm on my knees, praying about the thing that has me tangled up. Sometimes I'm on a run in the woods and a question bubbles up in my mind that doesn't feel like a question I would ask myself but more like something the God of the universe would ask. Or maybe it's not words at all but a visual of a person you know followed by the thought that you should probably text them and see if they're okay. Knowing it never hurts to reach out to a friend (and it's something Jesus would endorse), you type a message and hit Send.

Your friend texts back, "How did you know? I'm really struggling today. Thanks for reaching out."

I often get asked, "Do we ever hear God's audible voice?"

Some people do, but this is rare. And that's totally fine. I have tons of friends who have loved Jesus for decades and hear from God all the time but have never heard His voice out loud. There are so many other ways to hear from our loving Father.

I heard God speak out loud one time, and it was wild! God gave me a very specific three-word direction about a huge life decision we'd been praying about, when no one else was around except for my two-year-old daughter. And I promise, her voice wasn't that loud or that booming.

Try asking a trustworthy Christian friend or two to join you in your prayers for discernment or understanding or healing or a way out, or whatever it is you've been praying about. Sometimes God will give that friend a Bible verse or passage to share with you. God might give them a sentence or word He asks them to pass on to you. Or if you're looking for a job, they might actually know someone who's hiring.

If you're praying about something that affects your family or team or church, try praying together. Compare notes on what you hear. If multiple people feel God pointing in the same direction, that's helpful confirmation.

Don't forget that this isn't just about us getting answers to our questions from God. God often initiates the conversation. There might be times when you're just going about your life when God will speak to you. Because He wants you to know something or do something. It could be anything from the thought "Call your mom" to "Take the back roads instead of the highway" or even "Pray for the person next to you." *Really, God?* I sometimes ask. And He answers, "Who doesn't need prayer?"

The other day I was watering our fall flowers and one lone purple zinnia stood tall among canary yellow mums.

How did it get there? I hadn't planted zinnia seeds. Zinnia season was over. And wouldn't I have seen this plant while it was sprouting and growing prior to being in full bloom? It was a mystery, but it felt like God showing me that He is everywhere, full of beauty, and capable of anything. No words. No prayers. Just a lovely reminder from our heavenly Father of what He can and does do. That's God speaking.

One time the night before my husband and I left for a trip, Brett had a bad dream about us staying in the hotel he'd booked. Brett woke feeling strongly in his gut that we should avoid that hotel. And so we changed our plans. To this day we don't know why we weren't supposed to stay there. Nothing remarkable happened in the place where we did stay. To our knowledge nothing bad happened at the one we'd originally booked (we checked the news just in case). But because Brett fully believed God was warning him, we listened.

How might God be speaking to you today? I don't know for sure. But I do know that all the things He speaks are for our good and for His glory (Romans 8:28). That His words are full of love, grace, protection, and healing—like asking us to check in on a friend, share a Bible verse, drop a grudge, or fight injustice. When He wants us to hear something, He'll repeat himself or get louder if necessary. If we tune our hearts to Him, thrill on God's Word, talk to Him regularly, and drink His living water, we'll hear God speak.

And His voice will restore our souls.

PSALMS PLAYLIST

You can also access most of this music and more by searching for the playlist titled "Restore My Soul" by laurasmithauthor on Spotify.

Psalm 1: "Psalm 1" by Poor Bishop Hooper
Psalm 8: "Champion" by Dante Bowe
Psalm 23: "Psalm 23" by Holly Starr
Psalm 23: "Restore My Soul" by Vertical Worship
Psalm 23: "Shall Not Want" by Maverick City
Psalm 27: "Wait on You" by Maverick City
Psalm 40: "40" by U2
Psalm 42: "Satisfied in You" by The Sing Team
Psalm 42: "As the Deer" by Steffany Gretzinger
Psalm 89: "I Could Sing of Your Love Forever" by Delirious
Psalm 91: "His Wings" by Josh Garrels
Psalm 91: "On Eagle's Wings" by Shane and Shane
Psalm 96: "Psalm 96" by Vertical Worship
Psalm 104: "Jireh" by Maverick City
Psalm 118: "His Love Endures Forever" by Chris Tomlin
Psalm 121: "Another in the Fire" by Hillsong
Psalm 136: "Forever" by Chris Tomlin
Psalm 139: "Psalm 139" by Shane and Shane
Psalm 139: "I See You" by Jeremy Riddle

NOTES

1. Porter Anderson, "NPD: 'A Decade of Personal Exploration' Ahead in US Self-Help Books," Publishing Perspectives, January 17, 2020, https://publishingperspectives.com/2020/01/npd-sees-decade-of-personal-exploration-opening-usa-self-help-books/.

2. Jim Milliot, "Self-Improvement Boom Sets Book Sales Off on Fast Start in 2021," *Publishers Weekly*, January 14, 2021, https://www.publishersweekly.com/pw/by-topic/industry-news/bookselling/article/85316–book-sales-get-off-to-fast-start.html.

3. John Mark Comer, *We Don't Know What's Going to Happen and That's Okay: Living in Holy Uncertainty* (self-pub., 2020), 18.

4. Dr. Seuss, *How the Grinch Stole Christmas* (New York: Random House, 1957), 29–30.

5. Madeleine L'Engle, *Walking on Water: Reflections on Faith and Art* (New York: Crown Publishing, 2016), 162.

6. John Hughes, dir., *Ferris Bueller's Day Off* (Hollywood, CA: Paramount Pictures, 1986).

7. James Cameron, dir., *Titanic* (Hollywood, CA: Paramount Pictures, 1997).

8. Markham Heid, "You Asked: Is It Bad for You to Read the News Constantly?," *Time*, May 19, 2020, https://time.com/5125894/is-reading-news-bad-for-you/.

9. Annie F. Downs, "Getting Over Overwhelmed wk. 2 // Annie F. Downs // Cross Point Church // Message Only," CrossPoint.tv, October 16, 2017, video, 29:57, https://www.youtube.com/watch?v=8lEI51eNJRo.

10. Hudson Taylor, *Hudson Taylor's Choice Sayings: A Compilation from His Writings and Addresses* (London: China Inland Mission, n.d.), 51.

11. David Guzik, "Psalm 90: The Prayer of Moses in the Wilderness," Enduring Word, 2020, https://enduringword.com /bible-commentary/psalm-90/.

12. C. S. Lewis, *The Screwtape Letters* (New York: HarperCollins, 2001), 76.

13. Stacy Horn, "Singing Changes Your Brain," *Time*, August 16, 2013, https://ideas.time.com/2013/08/16 /singing-changes-your-brain/.

14. Ann Voskamp, "An Interview with NY Times Best-Selling Author Ann Voskamp," interview by Jason C. Dukes, Live Sent, May 9, 2011, https://livesent .com/2011/05/09/an-interview-with-ny-times-best -selling-author-ann-voskamp-one-thousand-gifts/amp/.

15. Maggie Masetti, "How Many Stars in the Milky Way?," *Blueshift* (blog), NASA, July 22, 2015, https://asd.gsfc.nasa .gov/blueshift/index.php/2015/07/22 /how-many-stars-in-the-milky-way/.

16. Karl Hille, "Hubble Reveals Observable Universe Contains 10 Times More Galaxies Than Previously Thought," NASA.gov, August 6, 2017, https://www.nasa.gov/feature /goddard/2016/hubble-reveals-observable-universe-contains -10-times-more-galaxies-than-previously-thought.

17. Rose Eveleth, "There Are 37.2 Trillion Cells in Your Body," *Smithsonian*, October 24, 2013, https://www .smithsonianmag.com/smart-news/there-are-372-trillion -cells-in-your-body-4941473/ .

18. C. S. Lewis, *Reflections on the Psalms* (Boston: Harcourt, 1958), 58–59.

ABOUT THE AUTHOR

Best-selling author and speaker **Laura L. Smith** speaks around the country sharing the love of Christ at conferences and events. She loves Jesus, her Prince Charming of a husband, their four kids, music, a good book, almond milk mochas, dark chocolate, and travel. Her dream spot? Sitting in a café in Paris with her family, drinking a café au lait and eating a pain au chocolat. Oh, and maybe when they all go to watch a soccer match, she'll sit and write. For hours.

She lives in the picturesque college town of Oxford, Ohio, where you'll find her running the wooded trails, strolling the brick streets, teaching Bible studies, shopping at the Saturday morning farmers market, or going on a sunset walk with her family. Visit her website at www.laurasmithauthor.com.

Help us get the word out!

Our Daily Bread Publishing exists to feed the soul with the Word of God.

If you appreciated this book, please let others know.

- Pick up another copy to give as a gift.
- Share a link to the book or mention it on social media.
- Write a review on your blog, on a book-seller's website, or at our own site (odb.org/store).
- Recommend this book for your church, book club, or small group.

Connect with us:

 @ourdailybread

 @ourdailybread

@ourdailybread

Our Daily Bread Publishing
PO Box 3566
Grand Rapids, Michigan 49501 USA

✉ books@odb.org